How to Archive
Family Keepsakes

How to Archive
Family Keepsakes

Learn How to Preserve Family Photos,
Memorabilia & Genealogy Records

Denise May Levenick
The Family Curator

FA MI LY
TREE
BOOK S

Cincinnati, Ohio

shopfamilytree.com

Contents

Introduction

THE ROLE OF THE FAMILY CURATOR

In every family, someone ends up with "the stuff." I had my first glimpse at a family archive when I was about seven years old. My elderly grandmother Arline held me by the hand to lead me into a shadowy back room that smelled of cologne and BENGAY ointment. She reached under a bureau and pulled out an old-fashioned suitcase, leaving a trail of dust on the wooden floor. I held my breath as she flipped open the metal latches, certain that great treasures would be revealed inside. But instead of jewelry or etched silver, all I saw was paper, paper, and more paper filling the interior.

Grandma sifted through the old letters, receipts, bankbooks, and loose papers until she found what she wanted to show me—a yellowing newspaper with screaming headlines. It was a news story about my grandmother and the brazen daytime child-snatching of her first daughter, my great-aunt Lucile. The suitcase filled with crumbling newsprint had taken on a whole new meaning; here was treasure after all.

I have always liked old things, so my grandmother's papers held a special fascination for me. Without any special fanfare or fuss, my family seemed to assume that I would be The Family Curator, the keeper of "the stuff."

By the time I inherited "Arline's Archive" in 2000, my grandmother had passed away, and all her papers had been moved to a large steamer trunk stored in a small, unheated office adjacent to my aunt's garage. Aside from the few days when I was allowed to borrow several items for a college paper, the trunk remained closed for thirty-five years.

When we finally lifted the lid of the large travel trunk, we saw absolute chaos inside. It looked as though someone had quite literally opened Grandma Arline's treasure-filled suitcases and dumped the contents into the large empty cavity of the trunk. There was no organization at all. Old photographs were lying next to bankbooks on top of letters, rent receipts, and blue chip stamps. Buttons, earrings, and metal curlers were mixed amongst the layers.

Most family archives aren't found in libraries or museums. Instead, like my grandmother's collection, they're found in suitcases, boxes, trunks, and drawers tucked away in attics, basements, garages, and even under beds.

Some storage places aren't bad environments for long-term storage, but many, especially attics and basements, are death zones for artifacts. The trunk had provided a relatively sealed environment for Arline's treasures, keeping things free from dust, damp, and vermin; but anything in the uninsulated room was subjected to the Southern California climate, which fluctuates from freezing to triple digits. Fortunately, the trunk must have been closed during dry weather; there was no trace of damp or mildew.

My first instinct was to sort and then store everything, but I learned that was not always the best way to work with a family archive. Organizing too soon can be as disastrous as poor storage. I certainly wasn't a professional archivist; I didn't even consider myself very good at organizing. I wasn't quite sure how to approach the project.

An entire life had been poured into a box and I needed help managing it. I wanted to know how to untangle the stories hiding in those documents, letters, and photos.

I set about learning best practices for working with historical materials, but couldn't find the information I needed. Genealogists were mostly concerned with organizing pedigree charts or preserving vital records; collectors dealt with artifacts like quilts, samplers, or military memorabilia; photographers focused on digitizing images. I learned something from each field, but I still wanted help working with an entire project.

The professional world of libraries and museums offered guidance in working with larger collections, which seemed closer to my goal, but they had knowledge, funds, and staffing that I didn't have. As I read more about archival practices, I discovered more questions:

What should I do first?

Should I sort or organize?

Should I move everything into archival storage?

Should I scan and digitize everything?

Should I make photocopies?

Should I keep everything?

What could I throw away?

I started using my word processor to keep notes on archival standards, how to care for various heirlooms, and what kinds of documents were important for genealogical research. Before long, I was drowning in information but still not making much progress in coming up with a realistic "game plan" to work with Arline's Archive. I knew what to do, but I didn't know how to begin.

On top of it all was the reality that I was a high school teacher with a busy family life. My grown sons were off at college and jobs, but home often enough that I wanted to be available for them and for our extended family. I helped my husband with office work for his business and enjoyed my volunteer commitments. My genealogy work was pretty well confined to school vacations and summers; I didn't have the time or resources to become a full-time archivist.

I was growing increasingly frustrated and discouraged, when I was struck by a true "aha" moment. I suddenly realized that I no longer thought of my inheritance as my "grandmother's stuff," but now looked at the contents of the trunk as The Arline Allen Kinsel Papers. My grandmother's things were just as much an "official" archive as any family history collection in the Smithsonian Museum.

Arline's letters, photos, and memorabilia all spoke of a fascinating story, but I didn't have to give up my life to be the permanent caretaker of her possessions. I found that by adapting professional methods for a family archive, I could confidently sort through my grandmother's treasures and discover the stories they held. I could more comfortably make decisions about items worth preserving and I could wisely invest the resources I had available for the project. I was in charge of the stuff instead of the other way around.

Since opening my grandmother's trunk, I have become The Family Curator for six more family archives. The largest included five homes filled with personal possessions; the smallest came in a brown paper lunch bag. I wasn't much different than the overworked museum staffers who have to decide how to handle hundreds of new collections. They couldn't possibly process everything immediately, so why should I expect that I could? I realized I could choose just how much sorting, organizing, and transcribing I wanted to do, and set my own timeline.

YOU AND YOUR FAMILY ARCHIVE

You may have boxes filled with treasures, or you may be helping a parent or relative downsize her possessions as she moves to a smaller home. You may even want help making your own family archive more accessible for your children and grandchildren. This book will help you organize your family archive and preserve your family history for future generations regardless of the size of your family history inheritance.

You probably have a busy life filled with many roles and responsibilities, so you don't need one more all-consuming project. You also don't need a lot of guilt simply because you choose not to spend your life caring for other people's possessions. That's why I've pulled together what I've learned to make your work as the family archivist as easy as possible.

HOW TO USE THIS BOOK

This book offers practical ideas for distributing items among family members, deciding what's worth saving, and preserving family heirlooms.

You won't need to spend hours searching books, websites, and articles to learn how to care for old documents or military ribbons; the first section of this book details basic care, organizing, and storage procedures for many of the most commonly inherited family history items.

You don't even need to rush out and spend a paycheck on archival supplies; you will find easy-working solutions that are also gentle on your wallet.

If you are organizing a sizeable family collection, I suggest you start at the beginning with chapter one and work your way through the ten checkpoints that help you organize your archive.

If you need quick answers for items that have landed on your doorstep, turn to chapters six, seven, and eight for ideas on care and storage.

It's essential that you move sequentially through the tasks, even if your archive is so small it can be contained in a shoebox. Otherwise, you may lose valuable clues and be sorry you rushed ahead.

When you're ready to move on, turn to Part 2: Break the Paper Habit to learn how to preserve your archive with digital master copies, and discover ways to make your research files and computer work more efficient.

Part 3: Root Your Research in Strategies for Success offers ideas for maximizing your research productivity and expanding your research, family connections, and family archive through social media.

Caring for family heirlooms is a rewarding adventure with hidden surprises; you never know what you may find.

I wish you many happy hours discovering the treasures in your own family archive. I'd love to hear about your experiences with the techniques in this book and the treasures you find; please send me a note at familycurator@gmail.com.

Happy archiving!

Denise Levenick
Pasadena, California

I Inherited Grandma's Stuff, Now What?

The expression "measure twice, cut once" is common in construction, but it's a notion that applies to working with your family archive as well. Careful planning now can save you hours and considerable anguish in the future. There is no "do-over" when it comes to the first time you open a box of family memorabilia carefully packed away by your ancestor.

Time spent planning now will help you create a firm plan to achieve an organized family archive.

Part 1 of this book will walk you through a ten-step plan to organize your archive. Be sure to complete each checkpoint in order.

Checkpoint 1: Organize Your Objectives (chapter one)

Checkpoint 2: Set Your Goals and Timeline (chapter two)

Checkpoint 3: Inventory Your Archive (chapter two)

Checkpoint 4: Order Your Storage Supplies (chapter two)

Checkpoint 5: Enlist Assistance (chapter three)

Checkpoint 6: Sort and Organize Your Archive (chapter four)

Checkpoint 7: Catalog Your Archive (chapter four)

Checkpoint 8: Find a Home for Your Archive (chapter four)

Checkpoint 9: Donate Your Family Archive (chapter five)

Checkpoint 10: Plan Your Legacy (chapter five)

1

Organize Your Objectives

A family archive is more than a scrapbook of old photos or a few boxes filled with trinkets inherited from your oldest relative. A family archive is part of an estate's personal property and may include:

- family photographs, slides, home movies, videos, or audiotapes
- portraits, miniatures, daguerreotypes, tintypes
- scrapbooks, baby albums, funeral memorial books, wedding albums, college yearbooks
- textiles, such as quilts, samplers, and heirloom clothing made by family members
- heirloom jewelry and watches
- heirloom furniture, clocks, rugs, etc.
- collections and collectibles, such as baseball cards or sports memorabilia, tools, teacups, toys, figurines, first edition books, cameras
- genealogical data, pedigree charts, research

A family archive is a collection of personal items. When a person passes away, these items become a part of her estate. Typically, personal items are not individually identified in a person's last will and testament, and the deceased may or may not have made provisions for the disposition of the family heritage items. Heirs are often unsure of how to handle these items, and you may be in this very situation.

A family archive can be inherited before death, as well. And it can be received separately from any other estate assets. Many times, a move to a smaller home or to a retirement community will prompt the current family curator to seek out a new home for the family memorabilia, often with someone in a younger generation.

An avid genealogist or local historian might even inherit an archive from a friend or acquaintance with a common interest and no suitable family members to receive the bequest.

In this chapter, Checkpoint 1: Organize Your Objectives will encourage you to name your collection and help you set goals and objectives for your family archive. If you are reading this book to get ideas for how to make proper provisions for your family heritage items, your descendents will surely thank you.

First, Save History

When it comes time to distribute personal property from an estate, first establish the family archive. Decide if you, or someone else, will be the "keeper of the stuff." When my aunt passed away, my interest in genealogy and family history made it a good fit for me to accept the family scrapbooks, albums, letters, and other "historical" materials. My sister and I were busy clearing out the house and getting it ready for sale, so anything "genealogical" went into boxes to be sorted later.

It's easy to spot many items of family history value, such as photos, letters, and albums, but what about the oddball things that may hold a clue to a family connection? If you are the genealogist in the family, don't be bashful about asking your relatives to be on the lookout for certain items that may be helpful in your research.

With any luck, the task of clearing out your relative's home will be shared by several family members. Ask your family to set aside anything they think might be useful; it's easier to throw it away later than lose the clue forever.

What Makes You Keeper of the Archive?

People who inherit family archives often take on one of three roles: the Curator, the Creator or the Caretaker. Look closely at each role. When you identify why you have the archive, it is easier to determine what to do with your inheritance. Whether you see yourself as Curator, Creator, or Caretaker, or maybe a blending of all three, you have inherited a wonderful opportunity to honor your loved one and create a lasting family legacy that will be a blessing, not a burden, for generations to come.

CURATOR

Curators have a good overview of the responsibilities involved in caring for a family archive—from organizing to preserving. Curators also know enough about the subject to recognize significant objects and suggest ways to use them in exhibits and collections. Consider that a professional curator understands what it takes to comprise a meaningful collection, as well as how to arrange, exhibit, and describe the collection so that visitors can take away a new understanding of the subject.

Likewise, a family curator looks for meaning in everyday objects, adds this to a family tree, drops in anecdotes and stories, and presents a snapshot portrait of a long-dead ancestor that others can relate to in the twenty-first century. The family curator then goes on to carefully preserve those objects, pedigrees, and stories so that our great-great-grandchildren will have access to the same family legacy.

CREATOR

A family history archive is an exciting resource for genealogy, scrapbooks, albums, films, and other creative projects. Even mass-market greeting cards have found uses for vintage family photos. Creative opportunities are everywhere.

If you plan to use a family archive in a creative endeavor, take time to research copyright laws and to obtain any necessary permission from other family members. Ownership of an item does not automatically give you the right to use or reprint an original work.

The women in my family are avid letter writers, and I have inherited a great deal of correspondence. According to United States Copyright Law, however, those letters are not mine to reprint or publish until they fall into the public domain. This date depends largely on the date of creation. Until then, the rights belong to the authors or heirs of the authors.

My grandmother Arline corresponded with many friends and relatives and she kept many of the letters she received. Even though those letters belonged to Arline and I inherited them, I cannot reprint them. The contents of those letters are just as protected as the content of any books I inherited from Arline. Fortunately, my grandmother inherited her mother's things, and her mother had kept many of the letters Arline had written her, so in a roundabout way, I did inherit many of Arline's letters, and because I am her legal heir, I am entitled to reprint and publish her works, no matter when they were created.

Creators should be aware of copyright laws affecting material found in a family archive.

The Curator's Commandment

Do No Harm

Think twice, if not three times, before attempting any conservation acts involving irreplaceable family artifacts. Ignore the torn scrapbook page, the loose photograph, the multi-page letter. Do not give in to the temptation to mend the scrapbook with tape, to glue down the loose photo, or staple together multiple pages.

Transparent tape, plain glue, and metal staples are archival enemies. All eat away at the surface of the item they are meant to repair and leave stains, tears, and marks when removed. Do not use tape, regular glue, or staples on family history materials.

Be certain that you have the legal right to print or reuse the work before publishing or using it in another form. Sharon DeBartolo Carmack's *Guide to Copyright & Contracts* answers many questions about copyright issues for genealogists and writers. Check with an attorney if you are unsure of your right to use family materials.

Creators will find many ways to use a family archive in their projects—from inspiration, to raw materials, to information sources. Following are a few ideas.

Complete a Family Pedigree

Genealogists and family historians look to family archives for primary research materials to confirm data or help break down brick walls. You may want to learn more about the life of your loved one, or unravel a family mystery.

Use your family archive to focus on finding and preserving vital records, those bits of history that establish who you are and who you came from.

- Birth, baptism, confirmation records showing proof of birth and/or parentage. These might be certificates, announcements, or handwritten notes in a family Bible.
- Marriage licenses and certificates, newspaper clippings, wedding memory books, photographs with captions, military pension records, or a family Bible confirming spouse and marriage date.
- Death certificates, obituaries, funeral home cards, news clippings.
- Be sure to keep different records establishing the same fact. Close examination may reveal conflicting information you will want to resolve, and corroboration can add authority to your claim.

Use good citations to credit the source of your information; your pedigree chart or family history sketch is a creative endeavor based on fact.

Write a Biography

If you plan to write a biography, you will need to save as much as you can that might shed light on the lives of your ancestors, and organize it for future analysis. In addition to vital records to establish lineage, look for items that will put flesh on the bones of your family stories.

- Business and personal letters, theater ticket stubs, city phone books, and club directories will help you learn about your family's friends, activities, and community.
- Photographs, movies, and slides can be used to illustrate your book.
- Audio tape or sound extracted from videos can be used in digital presentations.
- Family artifacts, such as chinaware or quilts, can be photographed and included as illustrations.
- Chapters six through eight will guide you in organizing the material so you can extract information you need.

Assemble a Scrapbook

Are you an avid scrapbooker? Your family archive can yield wonderful material for a legacy album. Make your project more manageable by prioritizing your heritage projects. Decide if you want to assemble an album featuring your grandparents' lives, or if you'd rather make a family tree book for your children. Use your family archive to add visual interest to your story.

- Digitize original documents and photos and reproduce for your scrapbooks; preserve the originals in archival storage. See Part 2: Break the Paper Habit, for ideas on digitizing material to preserve originals intact.
- Look for items that are visually appealing and "tell the story." Old certificates can be scanned and reproduced for effective page displays.
- Paper ephemera can add atmosphere and interesting embellishments for all kinds of projects.
- 3-D objects can be photographed and included in scrapbooks.

Compile a Family Medical History

Advances in genetic testing and analysis continue to add new possibilities for family health histories. Your intimate knowledge of your ancestors' life spans, illnesses, and causes of death can provide a vital link in a generational health study. Use your archive to add information to your family health history.

- Look for information about illness, accident, cause of death.
- Learn how to develop a medical family tree.
- Find family genetic clues with DNA testing.

CARETAKER

Where would we be without the family history caretakers who have guarded our legacy for generations? Many caretakers dutifully take on the role—and all the boxes—out of respect for a loved one. Others pick up the responsibility because "someone's got to do it." The truth is, though, not everyone who inherits a family archive is happy about it.

Thoughtful, responsible caretakers maintain many family archives until the time when the next person in line throws everything into the trash or the charity collection barrel. In one swift move, families lose their documented heritage to eBay and antique stores, or the local dump.

If you became the Caretaker by default rather than choice, take heart, you don't have to bear this burden forever. Here are two options that will put the archive en route to its next destination.

Hold Your Archive in Trust for Future Generations

Parents often hope to pass on special objects from grandparent to grandchild as a token between generations. If you have no particular goals or purpose in mind, other than to carry out the job you've been given, your best solution may be to simply hold the items for the next family curator. You may not personally see value in the archive, but you recognize that the person who owned it valued it, and you may hope someone else will value it just as much.

Realistically, think about your family. Is there anyone now living who would be willing to assume responsibility for the family archive? Is there a young grandchild keen on family stories who might be a future genealogist? If so, think about preserving your archive for him or her. Move ahead to follow the Caretaker's Plan and add your wishes to your estate plan. You may not have direct heirs yourself, but what about a niece or nephew, or even a cousin? Any blood relation interested in family history might be thrilled to become the caretaker of your family archive. If this sounds like your situation, consider the Caretaker's Plan.

The Caretaker's Plan

- Follow the Curator's Commandment: Do No Harm.
- Focus on keeping the material in original order, and moving it intact into archival storage.
- Don't feel compelled to sort and catalog.
- Remove anything you come across that might damage the materials, and throw it away. Old perfume bottles, leaking ink pens, and rusty metal don't have a place next to paper or photographs.
- Plan for the future. Include provisions in your will naming an heir for the archive. As a backup, identify a research repository to receive the collection.

The Donation Option

If no one in your family is interested in Grandma's trunk, investigate options for donation to a historical society, museum, or library. You will have the most success if the person was notable in some way to your community, or if he or she owned especially interesting items.

- Do you have the resources to organize the archive before passing it on? A museum will be more interested in your items if they are sorted and labeled.
- Can you make a contribution toward the long-term care of your family treasures? Museums always welcome monetary contributions to assist in archival expenses.
- See chapter five for ideas in preparing your items for donation and selecting an appropriate repository.

Before donating your materials, consider what I call the One Box Archive.

THE ONE BOX ARCHIVE: Decide to keep one box of items for future generations. Before donating your archive, take time to look through the archive and pull out vital records and anything that would help establish your family lineage. Add captioned snapshots, letters, or other items to fill the rest of the box.

GIVE YOUR COLLECTION A NAME AND SET YOUR GOALS

As you start the organizing process, think about the overall arrangement of your archive. Museums and libraries use several levels of organization; you can too.

The first level of your archive is your overall collection—the entire content. Start thinking of your inherited archive in terms of an official collection. Give it a name. Famous examples include:

- the Charles M. Schulz Collection
- the Norman Rockwell Family Papers

In Checkpoint 1, name your collection and write a brief description that includes how you came to inherit the materials, the number of boxes, and the general type of items it includes. Then go on to determine your overall goals and objectives.

Congratulations! You have completed the first task in working with an archive. You've written the provenance of your archive by identifying the person who owned the materials, their relationship to you, and how and why you acquired them. And, you have also identified your own goals and objectives for the materials.

Not all tasks are this easy, but you are on your way to organizing your family archive.

Provenance

Prov•e•nance *noun*

1. the history of ownership of a valued object, often including the origin, date of manufacture or creation, and full description
2. an item's chain of ownership

TIME: 10 minutes

Take a few minutes to consider why you took on the job of family curator and what you hope to accomplish in the role. In a journal or on a word processor, write the following sentences and fill in the blanks with your own information.

On (date) _____ I inherited the belongings of (name) _____ who was my (relationship to you) _____ because _____ _____ .

I have named this collection _____

Number of boxes _____

General description of contents (unbound paper, books, notes, etc.)

_____
_____

My Goals for This Archive

I would like to (check all that apply):

☐ Distribute everything to other family members
☐ Distribute _____ to _____
☐ Sell whatever is marketable
☐ Donate items to a research institution
☐ Organize the materials
☐ Use the materials for _____ project
☐ Hold the materials for _____ (name of heir)
☐ I am not quite sure what I will do with the stuff, but right now I am willing to learn more and consider my options.

I Consider Myself to Be a:

☐ Curator
☐ Creator
☐ Caretaker

This form is available to download online at <**familytreeuniversity.com/familykeepsakes**>.

2

Organize Your Plan

Creator, Curator, or Caretaker—now that you have an idea of your overall objectives, it's time to lay out the strategy that will help you succeed. Like any project manager, a step-by-step plan will move you forward toward your goal in a sequence of tasks without that "oops, I should have done this first" setback. It will also help you accomplish your organizing goals in a reasonable time frame. If you are like most people who inherit a family archive, you have a full-time job, a busy family life, volunteer responsibilities, and other interests. You are probably not a professional archivist, librarian, or museum curator (although you may be!). It's not hard for "someone else's stuff" to quickly drain your time and energy, leaving you feeling resentful and frustrated. A plan will keep you on schedule and minimize frustration. You can work on organizing your archive when you have time and energy, knowing you will eventually finish the project.

In this chapter, you'll go through three more checkpoints:

Checkpoint 2: Set Your Goals and Time Line

Checkpoint 3: Inventory Your Archive

Checkpoint 4: Order Your Storage Supplies

You will be working with your archive, but you won't be reorganizing or rearranging it just yet. The three checkpoints in this chapter lay the foundation for your organizing work by helping you to set a plan, identify the scope of the project, and gather the materials that you will need.

DEVELOP A STRATEGY

A good plan requires three things:
1. a concrete goal
2. an assessment of available resources
3. a realistic schedule with deadlines

In checkpoint 2 you will identify each of these plan components.

Identify Your Objectives

In checkpoint 1, you wrote down your overall purpose for the archive; let's work with those objectives to create a project plan. Transfer your objectives to Checkpoint 2 and add specific ideas or objects.

For instance, if your objective is to "Donate items to a research institution," you might note: Donate great-great-grandfather's Civil War letters to a library. If you are aware of libraries that might be interested, note them as possible options.

List Project Resources

All project management includes a realistic assessment of available resources, such as manpower, funds, and information. The key word here is *realistic*. If you work full time and are a parent of young children, you may need to cut back your objectives or extend your time line to accommodate your situation. Retired seniors or full-time researchers may have more time available, but may choose to limit the number of hours they spend on archival projects.

PEOPLE. List your name and the names of any other family members who you think might be interested in working with the archive. In chapter three, you will find ideas for pulling in assistance and sharing tasks.

TIME. Next to each person's name, indicate the amount of time per week they might be able to contribute to the project.

FUNDS. Give an estimate of how much money you have available for archival supplies. Use dollar signs if you don't want to commit to figures. ($=low cost; $$=medium; $$$=expensive)

INFORMATION. Do you need to arm yourself with knowledge? Are you unsure of how to care for or store certain items? This book includes a detailed section on preservation and archival storage, with resources to help you locate further information. If you know you will be looking for places to donate artifacts, start collecting details on potential repositories. Likewise, make sure you know how to contact family members who might like to help with your archive or assume responsibility for some items.

Set Deadlines

If your entry hall or garage has been lined with boxes since the death of your grandmother, you may be ready to set a deadline of tomorrow! The size and scope of your archive will largely determine the time required to get everything organized and out of your living space.

If one of your main objectives is to make a photo book for an upcoming family reunion, use the reunion as a starting point. Figure out how much time you will need to create the book and have it printed: If you need one month, set your deadline one month prior to the reunion. Time management experts know that merely setting a deadline is the greatest motivator of all.

Use Milestones

What can you do if the reunion is in only weeks away? You know that you can't possibly organize the archive in a month, but you would still like to make that photo album. No problem. Set the photo book as a Milestone Goal, a mini-goal that moves you toward your overall objective but occurs sooner rather than later. In fact, this is probably the way most of us approach our work with a family archive.

I was in the midst of organizing my grandmother's papers when my mom became ill and passed away. We wanted to assemble a photo slideshow for the memorial service, but I had barely started to look through boxes of old family pictures. I set aside my "organizing," and narrowed my search to find photographs suitable for the memorial. The originals were scanned and returned to the boxes for "organizing" later. Don't let the archive control you; remember, you are in control of the stuff.

Milestone Goals are also useful as mini-deadlines for large projects that can seem overwhelming.

Project Creep

Project creep is especially devious with family archives; before you know it, objectives expand, and more and more time is required until progress stalls or stops completely. It's perfectly okay to adjust your objectives from time to time; but, adjust your resources accordingly and be realistic in your plans.

MAINTAIN ORIGINAL ORDER

You might be ready dive in and start sorting and organizing your archive without looking back. If this is you . . . *stop*! Remember the Curator's Commandment: Do No Harm. Those piles of papers and photos may seem completely disorganized; but in reality, there is no such thing as random order.

People categorize their things in many ways, from the simplest seemingly random piles, to elaborate filing systems. Your archive may be more organized than you realize. Personality, time available, resources, education, training, occupation, and family life all play a role in an

TIME: 30 minutes

My Family Archive Objectives

(Ex: Donate third-great grandfather's Civil War diary to a museum—Allen County? Vermont Historical Society? Other?

_____

_____

Resources

PEOPLE / TIME

(Ex: Dad / one Saturday per month)

_____ / _____

_____ / _____

_____ / _____

FUNDS

(Ex: Estate offered to buy any needed archival supplies! $$$)

_____   _____

_____   _____

INFORMATION

(Ex: Pasadena Historical Society is interested in local items from Gramp's printing business; talk to Lois in the Donations Office 626/123-4567)

_____

_____

_____

MILESTONES AND DEADLINES

Project / Milestone Deadline

(Ex: Memorial Slideshow / due September 25)

_____ / _____

_____ / _____

_____ / _____

Deadline

By _____ I would like to have my family archive organized and stored in a suitable location.

This form is available to download online at <**familytreeuniversity.com/familykeepsakes**>.

individual's organizational style. Some people think like office managers and file alphabetically and categorically, others sort by date or event, or even person. Any groupings at all can provide clues to unmarked or seemingly unimportant items.

Some of the most common groupings found in unprocessed family archives include grouping items by primary structure, such as the kind of material, date, or subject.

When items appear to be grouped at random, often a secondary scheme is at work. A death in the family may bring assorted photos out of different boxes and albums to assemble a collage for the memorial service, but the pictures may be returned to storage in one large packet. Likewise, baptism certificates are often needed for confirmation or marriage and may end up mixed in with other paperwork from that time.

> ## How is your archive currently organized?
>
> **Primary Scheme**
> 1. Format: photos, letters, bank statements
> 2. Item Date: broadly by year or decade, more tightly by exact date
> 3. Subject: person, place, event
>
> **Secondary Scheme**
> 1. Family Life Event: baby, graduation, marriage, death
> 2. Transition: new job, relocation, divorce, downsizing, new member of household, move to/from college
> 3. Disaster: fire, flood, hurricane, tornado, earthquake

Everything was a jumble inside my grandmother's trunk. Grandma Arline liked to stash her memorabilia in old suitcases, and it looked like, at one time, the contents of each suitcase and box had been dumped directly into the larger trunk. Since then, things had been sifted and stirred by her daughters until it looked like one large pot of paper stew.

By the time I inherited the archive, the contents had already been moved to five cardboard cartons (another family member wanted to keep the trunk), further mixing up the materials. Any original order or groupings seemed to be lost. But as I began to work through the boxes just to evaluate the scope of the materials, I saw small packets and groups that had remained miraculously intact—envelopes filled with photos from an event, letters held together by a ribbon, bank receipts stuffed into a savings account passbook. Each group gave additional meaning to the items.

My grandmother's archive appeared random, but it wasn't. The remnants of groupings and sets show me that, at one time, she had things at least partially organized in a system that made sense to her. When I found nineteenth-century cabinet card photographs of two children labeled by name and a news clipping about those same children, I could assemble the story my grandmother tried to preserve. With a bit more detective work, I eventually determined that the young woman pictured in a second photo with the same children was Arline's young cousin, the girl who had rescued the children from a winter blizzard.

DETERMINE SCOPE AND CONTENT

Now that you've considered the entirety of your archive and understand that its contents are not random, you can look through it to determine the kind and quantity of materials you are dealing with. Professional archivists might call this determining "Scope and Content."

It's time to open the trunk and see what's inside those boxes. The purpose of this preliminary survey is to get an overview of the size and scope of your archive. We won't be sorting or cataloging today. We will use this information to

- order archival storage containers
- evaluate any assistance needed
- determine condition of the materials
- estimate time needed for the project

(Text continues on page 29.)

CHECKPOINT 3: INVENTORY YOUR ARCHIVE

TIME: about 10 to 15 minutes per box (set a timer to help you work quickly)

You Will Need

☐ inventory sheet—download online at **<familytreeuniversity.com/familykeepsakes>**

☐ large, flat work surface (e.g., dining room table covered with a clean sheet or folding tables set up in a spare room)

☐ permanent marker

☐ paper or file cards for placeholders

☐ digital camera

☐ trash can

Inventory Your Archive Step by Step

It's important to keep the contents of each container in the original order; you can use clues from these groups later if you need help identifying people or dates. Work with one box at a time, unpacking the contents layer by layer, and then replace the contents in the same order.

Step 1: Unpack the Container

1. Cover a large flat surface with an old sheet.

2. Label each container that currently holds archive material numerically: 1, 2, 3, 4, etc.

3. Label four file cards or sticky notes with numbers 1 through 4.

4. Start with the container you labeled number 1. Place it on a corner of your work surface, and set the other boxes aside.

5. Place your numbered file cards along the table in a row. These will be placeholder cards to help you remember the order of the box contents as items are removed and replaced in the box.

6. Remove the top layer from the box and place the contents under Card #1. Consider a handful of items, about 3 to 4 inches, as one layer; but be careful to pick up entire envelopes, folders, or other groupings. Just pick up the layer and set it down without flipping, rotating, or sorting. The items might be anything from a stack of old letters to a smaller box filled with photos. Photograph layers as you work if you need a point of reference.

7. Remove the next layer and place it under Card #2.

8. Continue until the box is empty. A standard banker's box holds about four layers, but add more placeholder cards if needed.

You should have four or more separate piles on your table, under the numbered cards you prepared in Step 3.

Checkpoint 3 continued next page

Step 2: Inventory the Contents

1. Use a simple inventory sheet to list everything in the box. (Download a free inventory sheet from <familytreeuniversity.com/familykeepsakes>.
2. Identify the container you are working with by listing the number you assigned the container and a description of the container that includes its size and type (e.g., box, trunk, folder, etc.).
3. Start with the bottom layer (under Card #4), briefly summarizing the items you find. You don't have to be very specific, but if you come across something of particular interest, be sure to itemize it. (See the example on the Inventory Sheet sample below)

ARCHIVE NAME: _____ The Arline Allen Kinsel Papers _____

Container #	Container	Size S/M/L	Layer	Contents Summary	Note
1	BB		4	Genealogy pedigree sheet	Mostly photocopies
1	BB		3	4 High School Yearbooks	Save
1	BB		2	3 Envelopes filled with used postage stamps	Give to Ed's grandson?
1	BB		1	Old Christmas cards, unused stationery, some letters from friends	Sort, discard stationery
2	P	M		Asst. black-and-white snapshots; a few larger portraits	Bill's Army pix

Step 3: Repack as You Work

1. After you inventory one layer, replace it in the container exactly as you found it. Don't rotate, flip, or reorganize.
2. You will be repacking the container from layer number 4 to layer number 1 (in other words, from the bottom up).
3. When you are finished, you should have a good idea of what the box contains.
4. At the top of the inventory sheet, summarize the box contents.

Inventory Tips

- Use a kitchen timer to give yourself a time limit per box. Start with ten or fifteen minutes per box. As you become more comfortable, the job will go faster.
- Don't sort and rearrange the contents of each container.
- Summarize items: e.g., About 20 misc. black-and-white vacation snapshots; 3 pkgs photos and negatives; assorted business correspondence.
- Make note of important items, e.g., Grandma and Grandpa Smith's wedding album, Michael Clark's WWI discharge papers.
- Make note of items needing priority preservation.

Checkpoint 3 continued next page

CHECKPOINT 3: INVENTORY SHEET

YOUR ARCHIVE _____

Container #	Container	Size S/M/L	Layer	Contents Summary	Note

Key

Container: B = Box   BB = Bankers' Box   P = Plastic Bin   E = Envelope

This form is available to download online at **<familytreeuniversity.com/familykeepsakes>**.

PROPER STORAGE CONTAINERS

Now that you know the kind of materials you have, you can find or purchase containers that will help you properly preserve the items. Consider your budget and your goals. You may not have the resources to buy new containers for your archive. You might be able to find suitable containers already in your home. Follow these guidelines.

Quick List: Storage Solutions

BEST

- closets located on interior walls
- cupboards and cabinets with tight-fitting doors
- steel filing cabinets located in an office or living area
- polypropylene terephthalate (PET) plastic jars

GOOD

- metal foot lockers
- suitcases
- plastic blanket bags with built-in vents (safe for some items)

AVOID

- plastic bins of any kind (see The Problem with Plastics section later in this chapter)
- plastic garbage bags
- plastic containers made of polyethylene or polyvinyl chloride
- PVC storage of any kind
- closets with exposed or adjacent plumbing
- closets and cabinets in a kitchen or bathroom
- unheated, uninsulated attic, garage, shed
- basement (beware of flooding)
- old metal cookie tins

ARCHIVAL STORAGE OPTIONS

Box Enclosures

Your archive's first line of defense against damage and deterioration is the box you select for overall storage. Containers should meet a few basic requirements:

- durable and rigid enough to provide sturdy protection for the contents
- sealed on all corners with a tight-fitting lid and no holes, such as handles or vents

- the size and shape of the outer box container corresponds to the contents; a file folder box will accommodate 9" × 11 ½" folders, a smaller flat box will protect a stack of same-size 5" × 7" photographs
- book and pamphlet boxes closely fit the contents

Paper Enclosures

For boxes, folders, mats, and other paper storage enclosures, "archival-quality" includes a tri-fold definition:

- acid-free—no wood pulp products
- lignin-free, or low-lignin—lignin is a substance that can cause acid to form in storage containers
- buffered or unbuffered (unbuffered preferred for certain drawings and paintings)—buffered paper has an added ingredient to neutralize the buildup of acid over time

Look for items that meet all three requirements when shopping for storage containers for your home archive.

Plastic Enclosures

- preservation polyester, Mylar, Melinex 516
- polyethylene
- polypropylene

When selecting storage enclosures for photographs, choose paper and plastic materials that pass the Photographic Activity Test (PAT). Use polyethylene and polypropylene products that are uncoated and made without plasticizers.

We know that wood pulp hastens deterioration, so it makes sense to eliminate or isolate any wood-pulp materials in your collection. This includes newspapers and any items printed on newsprint. You should be able to identify newsprint by its appearance, most often yellowed, brown, and brittle. Newsprint is highly acidic in nature due to the wood pulp used in its production.

Cotton or rag pulp, however, has proven to be a long-lasting substance. The survival of many old family letters and documents attest to the stability of good old-fashioned rag paper.

Riker Mounts

Have you heard the buzz about low-cost Riker Mounts? These clear front display boxes have been around for decades and are sometimes called "butterfly boxes." They make anything inside look special, but beware. Typical Riker Mounts are not assembled with archival-grade materials. If you want the "Riker Mount look" for your family heirlooms, seek out specialty storage from an archival supplier. Select acid-free, lignin-free boxes with see-through lids. These containers are sometimes called artifact boxes, specimen trays, or window display boxes.

ARCHIVAL ABCS

Preservation is all about *slowing down* the effects of time. It's not possible to preserve materials for eternity at the original quality. The best we can hope to do is minimize deterioration and stabilize materials as much as possible.

The term *archival-quality* is used liberally by product manufacturers, and a product that is labeled "*acid-free*" doesn't automatically meet true archival standards.

What's the fuss about acid-free materials?

If you've ever seen a newspaper left out in the sun for a few days, you've seen the damaging effect light, air, and temperature has on paper made from acidic materials. Common newsprint is made from wood-based pulp products that are high in acid. Archival paper is made from cotton pulp and boasts a basic pH of 7 or higher.

IS ACID-FREE THE SAME AS LIGNIN-FREE? No. Lignin is a component of paper that can cause the formation of acid. Look for archival materials that are low-lignin or lignin-free.

DO MY STORAGE MATERIALS NEED TO BE BUFFERED? Acid-free and lignin-free materials gain even longer shelf life when combined with a buffering agent, such as calcium carbonate during manufacture. This buffer helps neutralize acids that form over time. Some items, such as blueprints, drawings, and some photos can be damaged by the buffering component; they are better stored in neutral, or unbuffered, enclosures.

DO PLASTIC SLEEVES AND ENVELOPES NEED TO BE ACID-FREE AND LIGNIN-FREE? The archival terms "acid-free" and "lignin-free" don't apply to plastic enclosures. Look for plastic products that pass the Photographic Activity Test (PAT). Archival plastic products include polyester, polyethylene, and polypropylene.

THE PROBLEM WITH PLASTICS

Many people mistakenly place their confidence in economical plastic bins for heirloom storage. Plastic is truly a wonder-material. It is lightweight, clear, waterproof, relatively inexpensive, and easily available. It can be a useful tool for storage under the right conditions. The bins do a great job keeping out dust, vermin, and moisture under average conditions, but they can also trap moisture inside where mildew and mold will quickly grow. Clear plastic stored on an open shelf is not a good choice for items damaged by exposure to light; however, a PET plastic container used to store something inside a closed box or closet might be a practical and suitable choice.

What should you do if the storage medium isn't perfect? Use the best available at the time, and change storage methods when and if a better solution is discovered. Present archival practices recommend some types of plastic for certain storage situations, such as toys and crafts, as well as photographs or documents where viewing is desired.

Archival Plastic Storage Solutions

When selecting plastic boxes, jars, bags, and envelopes, look for containers made from:

- polyester (Mylar)—archival material
- polyethylene (not recycled)
- polyethylene terephthalate (PET)

GOOD

- polyester (Mylar) envelopes and film are good for storing flat objects.
- polyethylene terephthalate (PET) is stable and provides a near-perfect unbreakable oxygen barrier; it's available in jars and containers.
- polyethylene film made from new materials contains the fewest additives possible; it's a good choice for wrapping 3-D objects, but it can leech additives.

AVOID

- generic plastics without identification of materials
- plastic cling wrap because it commonly contains chlorine
- polyethylene containers made from recycled materials because they allow moisture in as the containers age
- polyvinyl chloride containers because they release contaminants

ARCHIVAL STORAGE OPTIONS CHART

It is helpful to have some idea of how you want to organize your archive before you invest in too many boxes or folders. Typically, you will want to group materials by creator/author and by kind and size of material. For example, photographs should be stored with other photos of the same size, negatives should be stored together, and documents should be stored with other documents.

Storage cases are made from different materials; always look for items labeled PAT certified, acid-free, lignin-free, buffered. Current products include:

- barrier board
- gray stone corrugated board
- copolymer of polypropylene and polyethylene (Coroplast ™)
- Tyvek ™ laminated barrier board

Container/Product	Look for	Best for	Notes
Drop spine boxes	Acid/lignin-free buffered	Flat storage of same-sized items	Many available sizes and shapes
Vertical file boxes	Acid/lignin-free buffered	Letter and legal size archival file folders	Use spacers to keep folders upright
Specimen boxes	Acid/lignin-free buffered	Collections of individual objects	Available with compartments in many sizes
Map tubes	Acid/lignin-free buffered	Rolled maps, documents	Interleave with archival tissue
Newspaper boxes	Acid/lignin-free buffered	Oversized documents, newspapers	
Pamphlet folders	Acid/lignin-free buffered	Brochures, small directories, address books, soft-cover pamphlets	Clear front available to show contents
File folders	Acid/lignin-free buffered	Paper documents, correspondence, photos, miscellaneous	Keep letter with envelope in folder
Paper folder sleeves	Acid/lignin-free buffered	Keeping letters with envelopes; grouping paper or photos	Place up to ten paper sleeves inside file folder
Buffered tissue	Acid/lignin-free buffered	Interleave with artifacts; provide cushion and protection	
ered paper	Acid/lignin-free buffered	Notes, photocopies; to support fragile items	Place behind fragile items in plastic sleeves
Labels	Acid/lignin-free buffered	Labeling boxes	
tic sleeves	PAT tested Polyester Polyethylene Polypropylene	Photos; fragile items that need visibility	

Chart continued next page

Container/Product	Look for	Best for	Notes
Plastic negative sleeves	PAT tested Polyester Polyethylene Polypropylene	Film slides, negatives	
Corrugated plastic boxes	PAT tested Polyester Polyethylene Polypropylene	Economical archival storage	Many available sizes and shapes
Plastic resealable zipper bags	PAT tested Polyester Polyethylene Polypropylene	3-D artifacts	Wrap item in buffered tissue, then place in bag
Cotton fabric	Washed, white cotton or unbleached muslin	Protecting odd-sized items from dust and light	Use clean white sheets, pillowcases, or yardage

RESOURCES: ARCHIVAL SUPPLIERS

Suppliers of Archival Products

Brodart **<www.shopbrodart.com>** (888) 820-4377

Gaylord **<www.gaylord.com>** (800) 962-9580

Hollinger Metal Edge **<www.hollingermetaledge.com>** (800) 862-2228

For More Information on Selecting Archival-Quality Products

"Storage Enclosures for Books" leaflet and "Artifacts on Paper and Storage Enclosures for Photographic Materials" leaflet by Northeast Document Conservation Center **<www.nedcc.org>**

Sally Jacobs, The Practical Archivist **<www. practicalarchivist.com>**

CHECKPOINT 4: ORDER YOUR STORAGE SUPPLIES

TIME: 30 to 90 minutes

Archival-quality storage containers are the best options for preserving family treasures. These products are manufactured to meet current archival standards, and they are the same products used by museums and libraries worldwide.

Browse catalogs and websites from archival storage suppliers to get an idea of products, pricing, and ordering information. See Resources: Archival Suppliers in this chapter for a list of suppliers. Some companies offer a discount when ordering in quantity. Archival supplies are more expensive than office-supply alternatives, but they offer the best protection for your precious heirlooms.

All materials should be archival-quality. Look for acid-free, lignin-free, and buffered options. Plastic storage should be labeled that it passes the Photographic Activity Test (PAT).

You Will Need

- ☐ catalogs from archival suppliers or Web links to supplier websites
- ☐ completed Inventory Sheets from Checkpoint 3
- ☐ Archival ABCs information in this chapter
- ☐ Archival Storage Options Chart
- ☐ Archival Supply Shopping List

Make a List to Order Your Storage Supplies Step by Step

1. Carefully read your Inventory Sheets and list the kinds and quantity of items you will need to store on the blank Archival Supply Shopping List.
2. Review supplier websites and catalogs to view various containers and compare prices. For most materials, you will need individual enclosures made of paper or plastic and archival boxes. Avoid placing items in boxes without individual protection, if possible. Decide what kinds of enclosures and boxes you prefer and tally the quantity and cost.
3. Order storage containers.
4. Review the Archival Supply Shopping List for other items you may need, such as white cotton gloves for handling photographs and fragile documents, a marking pen, labels, etc.
5. Remember to order acid-free tissue to cushion fragile artifacts and labels for storage boxes.

Checkpoint continued next page

Tips

- Measure shelf height in your prospective archive location. Determine if vertical or horizontal storage boxes will best suit your space.
- Consider storing documents and photos in hanging folders inside a metal filing cabinet.
- You may want to order a sample of several products before deciding which you prefer.
- Use boxes of uniform size as much as possible.
- Order in quantity and watch for special sales to save money.

CHECKPOINT 4: ARCHIVAL SUPPLY SHOPPING LIST

Note: All storage containers should be archival-quality.

This form is available to download online at **<familytreeuniversity.com/familykeepsakes>**.

I Have [number]	Items I Need to Store	How to Store	Container	Qty to Buy	Cost
	Standard-sized documents	Vertical storage: Paper file sleeves inside file folders inside document cases	Paper sleeves		
			File folders		
			Document cases		
	Odd-sized (large or small) documents	Flat storage: inside Mylar or paper folders inside drop spine boxes	Mylar or paper folders		
			Drop spine boxes		
	Correspondence	Vertical storage for many letters; flat storage for a small collection. Open letter and place flat inside paper file sleeve or file folder with envelope.	Paper sleeves		
			File folders		
			Document cases or drop spine boxes		

I Have [number]	Items I Need to Store	How to Store	Container	Qty to Buy	Cost
	Photographs	Sort by type and size; place in plastic or paper sleeve and store vertical, flat, or in three-ring notebooks	Plastic or paper sleeves		
			Photo boxes or photo binders		
	Newspapers	Always store separate from other items; open and store flat	Large newspaper folders		
			Large newspaper boxes		
	Pamphlets and small books	Pamphlet folders stored flat; multiple folders inside drop spine box	Pamphlet folders		
			Drop spine boxes or book boxes		
	Scrapbooks containing various items	Store separate from other items in pamphlet folder or book box	Pamphlet folders		
			Drop spine boxes or book boxes		
	Photo albums	Pamphlet folders stored flat inside drop spine box	Pamphlet folders		
			Drop spine boxes or book boxes		
	Artifacts	Wrap lightly in archival tissue, and store in suitable-sized container	See chapter eight for specific storage options.		

3

Organize Assistance
from Family Members

Family stories play a leading role in deciding the difference between trash and treasure in a personal estate. A funny wooden plaque that hung in my mother-in-law's kitchen for decades was a hotly-contested item when the grandchildren were invited to make selections from her home. On the other hand, a beautiful and valuable European clock had no takers. Everyday items can help us recall a special memory. The chipped batter bowl may bring to mind winter afternoons baking cookies with your grandmother; the old chisel can tell stories of dad's repair shed.

Family historians and those named as Executors or Trustees are often the eldest children in the family. We are more accustomed to giving help than asking for assistance. But when it comes to distributing the personal property of a loved one, we may be surprised to find ourselves caught in the emotional fallout of complicated family relationships. If I could offer one bit of advice for dealing with an estate, it would be this: Act slowly and carefully. There is no big rush here. Your beloved grandmother, uncle, or parent has passed away and nothing will change that hard fact. Life will not be measurably better by quickly disposing of their personal effects just to "move on." Death is pretty final, but the stuff left behind can continue to haunt family relationships for generations.

The way you choose to handle what remains from your loved one's life—the trinkets as well as the treasures—is an opportunity for you to help build long and loving memories within your family. As the Executor or Curator, you can do a great deal to build your family legacy through the decisions you make as you handle your loved one's estate.

Act thoughtfully and respectfully when it comes time to distribute personal items. Each person who knew your loved one had a completely unique and independent relationship with that person and with his or her belongings. Respect these relationships when deciding how to dispose of personal items. Your job as Executor is to facilitate the distribution of property; you don't have to give up your own life to manage someone else's life possessions. Even as Curator, you are merely holding things "In Trust" for future generations. Consider your task as Executor as an honor from your loved one and an opportunity to strengthen family ties.

APPOINT FAMILY CARETAKERS

Resist the temptation to do everything yourself. Yes, it may be faster, easier, and more expedient, but it can also lead to resentment and hard feelings among family members. Personal items often act as "memory triggers" helping us recall an event, person, or place. Try to find a balance between efficiency and emotions, even if it means a delay while you ask young cousin John, the sports fan, if he would like to be the caretaker of his grandfather's athletic equipment.

My aunt enjoyed quilting and we often exchanged patterns and tips. My sister and aunt attended the same church and liked to share stories and photos about the community "now and then." After my aunt passed away, my sister accepted the local scrapbooks and memorabilia; I took home the sewing supplies and quilting patterns. We each sorted through the boxes, selecting what we wanted to keep. Then we took care of donating or discarding what was left. My sister kindly scanned photos and documents I wanted to include in my genealogy records. I found a few handmade items I passed back to her for her granddaughters. Auntie's mementos and crafts found new homes where they are cherished and enjoyed.

Some items, of course, you will want to keep intact as a collection, especially genealogical or family history papers. Other items may be most meaningful to a particular family member who holds a special connection or memory with that item.

My father-in-law was a career Army officer and a graduate of the United States Military Academy at West Point. The eldest grandson requested his grandfather's West Point diploma and the framed document is now handsomely displayed in his home office; digital copies keep the information available for genealogy files.

The benefits of sharing responsibility for family treasures with others include:

- less for you, as Executor, to personally sort and store
- a greater sense of shared responsibility for the family history
- a better understanding of the family legacy
- more family members learn how to properly care for family treasures

WHO CAN BE A FAMILY CARETAKER?

Your twenty-something cousin doesn't need a degree in Archival Practices or Library Science in order to become the caretaker of his grandfather's baseball cards. The most important criteria is a shared interest in family history and baseball cards, followed by the proper place to store the items. It might not be a good idea to give the cards to Cousin Tom if he plans to take them with him to college. Instead, purchase archival boxes and ask him to store them in his bedroom closet at home.

Listen to your instincts and rely on your knowledge of people and personalities when deciding to share family treasures. Look for a good fit between interest, stability, and accessibility.

The ideal family caretaker is:

- personally interested in the item itself, whether baseball cards or cookbooks
- able to provide long-term archival storage
- willing and able to provide any additional insurance deemed prudent
- willing to share the item or collection with interested family members for viewing or copying
- willing to keep family members informed of the location and status of the collection

FAMILY COLLECTION SHORTLIST

Here's a shortlist of the kinds of items that are well-suited to being divided among family members as "mini-archives":

- high school and college scrapbooks, yearbooks, memorabilia
- athletic gear and/or memorabilia
- sports collections (baseball cards, game programs, team memorabilia, etc.)
- military medals, certificates, and memorabilia
- heirloom textiles, such as quilts or samplers
- cookbooks or other book collections
- photographic slides and/or home movies and video
- the family Bible
- heirloom family photo albums or scrapbooks
- portraits, paintings, other art
- furniture
- collectibles and whole collections

WHAT TO DO WITH. . .?

Some things found in a typical estate should be handled with extra thoughtfulness. Avoid hurt feelings among family members by following a few guidelines.

Gifts From Family Members

Return gifts to the giver, especially expensive or rare items. It isn't practical to do this for everything, but it is certainly thoughtful to return an expensive painting or piece of jewelry to the person who presented it as a gift. Allow the gift-giver to decide whether to accept the item or keep it in the estate for distribution among family members.

Personalized Items

Mothers and grandmothers often receive gold or silver charms engraved with the name of their children or grandchildren or set with birthstones. Consider giving each of the children or grandchildren their special charm. If the bracelet or necklace was a gift, return it to the giver as well.

Personal Correspondence and Greeting Cards

Whether they are letters from college, Army days, or between friends, by law the letters are copyrighted by the author. It is respectful to return letters to the writer when practical. Grown children often enjoy seeing the handmade cards they sent their grandparents and knowing that the cards were treasured over the years.

Bequests

Nowadays, people rarely include personal bequests in their Will or Trust; however, you may find a list or notes for dispersing certain items. My mother tucked notes inside china, behind pictures, and inside jewelry boxes describing what things meant to her and who she wanted to inherit them. We honored her wishes by passing on those items to friends and family.

EDUCATING THE CARETAKERS

As you share responsibility for family treasures with others, take time to share a few guidelines for proper storage and handling. Make the task easier by providing archival storage containers or funds from the estate to purchase what is needed. Include the following Quick Guide for Family Caretakers.

QUICK GUIDE FOR THE FAMILY CARETAKERS

These tips will help identify where and how to store family treasures. When taking on this job, think like Goldilocks:

- Not too hot, not too cold. Not too wet, too dry, or too buggy. Look for a place that is "just right."
- Interior closets and cupboards are great. Avoid attics, basements, and garages where temperature fluctuations can cause damage quickly.

Keep Similar Things Together

- Store paper, books, and photos together. Do not mix with metal (it can rust) or liquids.
- Keep newspapers and cardboard completely separate from other objects.

Go Natural

- Use acid-free, lignin-free archival boxes and folders.
- Use old cotton sheets as a buffer to keep out dust.
- Wash your hands before handling paper and photos, or wear white cotton gloves.

The Problem With Plastic

- Some plastics leech chemicals that can damage contents.
- Plastic traps moisture inside containers causing mildew and mold.
- Review the Quick List: Storage Solutions in chapter two for guidelines in using plastic storage containers.

CHECKPOINT 5: ENLIST ASSISTANCE

TIME: 60 minutes

If you would like help but are unsure who would want the items, send out a brief but clear family letter. Use the following example as a model for your letter.

> *Dear Family,*
>
> *Grandma Mary left us with a wonderful family and a legacy of memories. She also left us with many family treasures. I hope that you will share the family legacy by agreeing to act as caretaker for some items that may hold a special connection for you.*
>
> *I am attaching a list of the kinds of items that need a new home within our family. Your responsibility will be to help sort the items and decide what to save, and to provide suitable storage. The estate will provide funds to purchase any archival storage containers needed and everyone will receive an inventory so that we know "who has what."*
>
> *Please contact me by Saturday, October 1st if you would like to become a Smith Family Caretaker.*
>
> *Love, Aunt Jane*
>
> *LOOKING FOR A NEW HOME*
> - *High school and college yearbooks—12 volumes*
> - *Grandpa Maynard's records and sheet music—2 boxes records, 1 box sheet music*
> - *Photo Gear—every camera, projector, and viewer Grandma and Grandpa owned, about 5 boxes. (We could also use some help reviewing several boxes of old slides and old movies!)*
> - *Grandma's cookbook collection—4 shelves worth*
> - *Family Christmas cards—2 large boxes*
> - *Political buttons, bumper stickers, etc.—1 box*
> - *Uncle Joe's scrapbooks from his sports days at the University—4 books*

4

Organize Your Archive

Your archival supplies have arrived. You've managed to set aside a block of time to go through your family archive. You've made a preliminary inventory, but until now, you've resisted reading letters, analyzing documents, and taking a closer look at old photographs. At last, it's time for the real nitty-gritty of discovering just what is inside all those boxes. Your patience is about to pay off, and by the end of your first archiving session, I hope you feel a great sense of accomplishment.

In this chapter, you will be moving materials into archival storage containers, preparing a catalog to help you find things, and moving your containers to an appropriate location in your home. Continue to work through each checkpoint in order as you organize your archive:

Checkpoint 6: Sort and Organize Your Archive

Checkpoint 7: Catalog Your Archive

Checkpoint 8: Find a Home for Your Archive

WHAT TO SAVE? WHAT TO KEEP?

Genealogists and family historians can have a hard time throwing things away when it comes to the bits and pieces of our ancestors' lives. We are looking for clues to confirm identity, establish lineage, and solve family mysteries. We hope to find stories and personal anecdotes that will bring our ancestors to life and help us feel connected to our past. Look to photographs, letters, and documents for written details that may be useful in pedigree charts, ancestor sketches, and family histories. As you sort through your archive, be on the lookout for family history along the paper trail.

Don't overlook artifacts; my mother routinely tucked notes inside vases and taped letters to the back side of framed artwork that described the item and chain of ownership. You will want to make decisions about knickknacks and other things as you work through the box. Whether or not you decide to keep a ring of rusting old keys may depend more on your interest in antiques than in your archival strategy.

This is also the time to remove anything that might damage other items. Rusting metal, leaking perfume bottles, food, or other bits of debris should be isolated or discarded.

STEP 1: IDENTIFY WHAT YOU WANT TO DO WITH THE OBJECT

You have five options for what you can do with an item:

1. Keep it.
2. Give it to a relative or friend.
3. Donate it.
4. Sell it.
5. Throw it away.

STEP 2: SORT THE MATERIAL INTO STACKS

As you sort, create separate groups for items you will donate, sell, and give to family members (clearly label each pile so you don't forget). If you know who you will give the item to, create separate, labeled piles for each family member.

When it comes to the keep pile, you need to decide how you want to rearrange the collection for future storage. What's the best way to arrange and group the items? Ultimately, you will need to decide what organizing method works best for your purposes. (Remember Checkpoint 1 in chapter one?)

Archivists recommend preserving *like with like*. The original cartons may have contained a mix of photos, documents, and letters about different events, or a complete jumble of different materials and artifacts. In this method, you will sort items by kind, size, and shape. For example, store all 5" × 7" photographs in a 5" × 7" box. This method provides stability and prevents larger items from scratching, crushing, or damaging smaller ones.

There's only one problem: by regrouping items, you can lose the sense of original order. If you are trying to preserve the story of the items, you may want to leave things grouped together. You will have to use your best judgment to retain the context of the material.

Sorting Strategies

- Use the Sorting Quick List in this chapter as a guide to help you decide whether an item is worth saving or not.
- Try to handle things only once. Pick up an item, decide, and move it to the appropriate pile.
- Keep grouped items together; do not break up packets or collections.
- Select ephemera to save for scrapbooking projects if you have a use for them.
- Remove metal such as paper clips, staples, and wire; you will probably see signs of rust where metal has come into contact with paper or fabric.
- Remove rubber bands, ribbons, and other ties; place items together in an archival folder.
- Isolate newsprint flyers and newspapers to store separately.
- Pay attention to the quality of paper. If you suspect a high-acid or lignin content, test with a pH pen and isolate the material in a separate archival envelope or sleeve.
- Look for signs of mold, mildew, or insect damage and note it on your inventory sheet.
- Brush off loose dirt, note damage or needed repair.
- Use envelopes to hold items you may wish to give to a family member or place in a different box.

Here are three options to consider when working with photos and documents of varying sizes:

1. ORIGINAL GROUP. Protect each item by enclosing it in an individual archival sleeve or folder and then placing the group inside a box or folder maintaining the original group. If the items are all of the same kind, such as all color snapshots or all correspondence, you might like to keep everything intact and just move it to an archival container. Many times it makes more sense to maintain the original packets and groups.

2. CATEGORY. Determine categories, such as person, date, or event. Enclose each item in individual archival sleeves or folders and then place the items in a box or folder sorted by category.

This method can be helpful if you are trying to assemble material for a project focused on a specific person or event. To keep a record of the items' original locations, make a note on your Inventory Sheet listing the former box number.

3. KIND AND SIZE. Sort items by kind (e.g., photo, letter) and size. Place items in individual sleeves, and group in an appropriate-sized container. Separate by person, date, or event within this larger container using archival dividers. For example, place all 5" × 7" photos in one box, all 3" × 5" photos in another box. Within each box, you could group photos of an event or a person together and keep groups separated by an archival index card.

If your archive includes a great number of same-sized photos or documents, this can be a good solution that organizes by person or event within a larger group.

Whatever organizing method you decide to use, feel free to adapt your storage to suit your purpose. You might have hundreds of old black-and-white snapshots and just a few other

CHECKPOINT 6: SORT AND ORGANIZE YOUR ARCHIVE

TIME: about 30 minutes per box

To begin the project, set aside an afternoon or block of time when you will be uninterrupted and can spread out your materials on your workspace.

You Will Need:

☐ a clean flat workspace (cover the dining table with a clean sheet)
☐ white cotton gloves for handling loose negatives, jewelry, photos, documents
☐ Inventory Sheets completed in Checkpoint 3
☐ archival labels
☐ archival marking pen
☐ archival storage containers ordered in Checkpoint 4
☐ a trash container
☐ several large envelopes (archival preferred)
☐ appropriate archival storage containers

Sort and Organize Step by Step

Using the same step-by-step process you used to inventory the boxes, work one box at a time as you remove each item from its box:

1. Identify what you want to do with the object.
2. Place it in the appropriate stack.
3. Move items to archival storage, donate, give away, sell, or throw out.

Sorting and Storage Tips

1. Refer to chapters six, seven, and eight for best practices in storing materials.
2. Prepare the items for long-term storage by discarding paper clips, staples, etc.

This form is available to download online at **<familytreeuniversity.com/familykeepsakes>**.

Sorting Quick List: To Keep or Not to Keep

SAVE

vital records

graduation, baby, marriage invitations and announcements

educational records—school report cards, school photos

military records—discharge papers, letters, awards

Christmas cards and envelopes

Christmas card list

recipes, handwritten favorites

address books

bank passbooks

income tax returns

journals, diaries, ledgers

scrapbooks, autograph albums, photo albums

correspondence

employment records—pay stubs, contracts, résumés (keep enough to verify employment and salary)

telephone books

city and club directories and rosters

genealogy and family history charts, narratives, family trees

SKIM, THEN TRASH

church and club newsletters—skim for family news, save a representative copy

cancelled checks, check registers—skim for heirloom purchase, cost of living expenses

news clippings—skim for news of family or friends

travel itineraries and brochures—skim for information on trips or places where relatives might live

old calendars—skim for birthdays, anniversaries

receipts—skim for heirloom purchases, auto registration (extract make, model, license)

medical bills, records—extract information

TRASH

random newspaper and magazine clippings

bank statements

old insurance policies

travel brochures

odd-sized photos. Consider storing the snapshots together in a suitable-sized box and the odd photos divided up into folders by family, person, or date.

STEP 3: MOVE ITEMS TO ARCHIVAL STORAGE, DONATE, GIVE AWAY, SELL, OR THROW OUT.

After you finish sorting the contents of a box, select the appropriate archival container for each item. You can add to these containers after you finish sorting each original box or container in the archive.

The hard part is behind you, now all you have to do is distribute the items where they belong. Throw out the melting candles and old candy bars, take the box of gadgets to the thrift store, list the teacups no one wants on eBay, and give your uncle the baseball ticket stubs. After you've taken care of everything you don't want to keep, take a good look at what remains.

You may need to further sort photos and documents, depending on the contents of other boxes. You should have a good idea of the quantity of each item you need to store. Select appropriate-sized containers and begin moving your materials to their new home.

Photos can scratch easily when handled; consider enclosing prints and negatives in archival plastic or paper sleeves. Place documents and letters inside file folders. These individual items should be placed inside an archival box, creating yet another barrier against environmental damage.

If your archive is large and you are working through materials one box at a time, it may take you several sessions to transfer items from old boxes into new archival storage. You may need to work with three or more containers at once: a document case for papers, a drop spine box for large photos, and another flat box for pamphlets. Just add to the boxes each time you sort through another box.

STEP 4: CREATE A CATALOG

The time you invest in this step will be returned to you in the future when you need to find something in your archive. It's decision time, again! How much time do you have to devote to cataloging your archive? Professional archivists like Sally Jacobs, The Practical Archivist, understand the time and funds required to develop a comprehensive collection catalog. If your archive is quite large, you may not want to take the time at this point to individually list each item. Use a general descriptive term, such as "Kansas farm—photos, documents" to help you locate the items as needed. Sally advises home historians to start with the box-level description and then move on to the folder-level description before getting overwhelmed by the specifics of item-level descriptions.

Aim for a minimum summary of what's inside the box; you can go back and itemize folder specifics when you have time. Include names, years, and events when known.

TIME: about 30 minutes per box, depending on your level of detail

You Will Need

- ☐ Catalog Form (in this chapter)
- ☐ Archive Index (in this chapter)
- ☐ archival paper
- ☐ three-ring binder

Catalog the Contents of Your Archive Step by Step

1. Label your new archival storage boxes by number and note these numbers on your catalog form.
2. Complete the catalog entry for each box as it is filled.
3. Make a copy of the catalog form on archival paper.
4. Place your copy inside the box on top of the contents.
5. Assemble a three-ring binder with another copy of the catalog form for each container.
6. Copy the container numbers and summaries from your catalog form to an Archive Index.
7. Place the Archive Index in the front of your three-ring-binder.
8. Make copies of your catalog for interested family members.

Your Archive Catalog

Complete one form per box. Copy the completed form and store one copy inside each box on top of the contents. Place a copy in a three-ring binder with all catalog sheets for your archive. Transfer the summary to the Archive Index and keep it in the front of your binder.

Computer Version: Make your list searchable and easily edited by keeping the catalog on a spreadsheet or database. Print updates regularly and keep a hardcopy in the box and in a binder for easy reference. Your descendants may not have access to your computer; make it easy for them to find your material.

This form is available to download online at <**familytreeuniversity.com/familykeepsakes**>.

CATALOG FORM

Your Archive				
Archive Box #		**Date Cataloged**		
Summary of Box Contents				
Folder #	**Description**	**Years**	**Quantity**	**Notes**

This form is available to download online at **<familytreeuniversity.com/familykeepsakes>**.

SAMPLE CATALOG FORM

Your Archive		Arline Allen Kinsel Papers		
Archive Box #	Box 1	**Date Cataloged**		12 Aug 2012
Summary of Box Contents		Chamblin Correspondence, Photos, Documents 1909-1942		
Folder #	**Description**	**Years**	**Quantity**	**Notes**
Folder 1	Sam Chamblin's correspondence	1909-1942	45-50	Good condition; originally scattered in several boxes
Folder 2	Photographs of Sam Chamblin	1923-?	15	
Folder 3	Military service papers and snapshots taken during tours of duty	1914-1919	8	
Folder 4	News clippings about accidental death of S.C.	1942	3	

This form is available to download online at **<familytreeuniversity.com/familykeepsakes>**.

ARCHIVE INDEX

Archive Index for (name of your archive) _____

Located at _____

Now in the possession of _____

Archive Container #	Summary of Contents	Date Cataloged

This form is available to download online at **<familytreeuniversity.com/familykeepsakes>**.

Your nicely organized archive won't be much use if you can't locate items when needed. You don't need a complex or deeply detailed system to be able to use your materials; even museums and libraries use a general, box-level system for many collections. A simplified catalog system will provide a box-by-box inventory and the basic structure for a more detailed itemization in the future. Create your catalog by numbering each folder, box, and container in the collection. Then list the contents of each under the appropriate number. If you keep your catalog in some kind of computer system, you will have the added ability to search easily and quickly for any materials you need. See chapter ten for ideas on scanning and preserving digital versions of your heirloom documents and photos.

FINDING A SAFE HOME FOR YOUR ARCHIVE

Your family heirloom photos, documents, and letters are finally organized and stored in archive-quality containers. Now where do you put those containers so they remain safe from damage? "Everything you love and own eventually falls apart," writes Don Williams, Senior Conservator at the Smithsonian Institution. "The best way to ensure that stuff lasts is to place all your collectibles in an Egyptian tomb and then seal them in," he adds. "No light, no humidity fluctuation, no contaminants, no bugs, no furry friends, and no people." These are perfect conditions for preservation.

Most of us aren't quite ready to stash our stuff in an Egyptian tomb, or rent space in a temperature-controlled bank vault. We are looking for a *practical, feasible,* and *economical* storage solution for our family treasures, and, if you are a family historian or genealogist, you might want to add *accessible* to your storage requirements.

From Trunk to Archive

While I store some things in my heated basement, I store my grandmother's photos, letters, and memorabilia in my "best" storage location, which is upstairs in my house. Grandma Arline's Archive had also been stashed in an old-fashioned steamer trunk that looked as if it may have once moved someone across the country.

Arline's trunk provided a closed environment to protect the contents. Unfortunately, the trunk had lived for over thirty years in an unheated room attached to the garage. Summertime temperatures surely pushed into the triple digits and winter chills dropped to freezing, even in Southern California. The best you can say is that while the trunk's contents may have suffered from humidity and temperature fluctuations, they were fairly secure from those other archival enemies—air, light, dust, pests, and people.

After assessing the contents and ordering archival supplies, the contents of Arline's trunk were relocated to archival storage boxes that now live in my living room bookcase cabinets. Right now, everything is easily accessible for transcribing, indexing, and scanning. Of course, there is a bit of an overflow with oversized boxes and folders, as well as materials from other family members. Sturdy shelving in a guest room closet serves as a second family archive: labels keep the boxes in order, and an Index helps me locate materials as needed.

You don't have to have an entire room dedicated to archival storage in order to be the curator of your family's memories. Do the best with what you have. Consider your options, be creative, and remember that you can relocate and upgrade storage as time, funds, and information change. Nothing is forever. Your efforts can only slow down—not eliminate—the effects of time. Just do your best.

CHECKPOINT 8: FIND A HOME FOR YOUR ARCHIVE

TIME: 30 to 60 minutes

You Will Need

- ☐ completed Archive Index from Checkpoint 7
- ☐ completed Catalog Forms from Checkpoint 7
- ☐ three-ring binder

Finding a Home for Your Archive Step by Step

1. Walk through your home and identify a good storage location for your archive. If space is an issue, you may need to keep boxes in a few separate locations.
2. Clear out the designated locations.
3. Move the archive to the designated locations.
4. Mark the location of each box on your Archive Index and the catalog page so you can quickly find boxes in the future.
5. Assemble all Inventory Sheets and the Archive Index in the binder and keep them with the archive. Keep a duplicate set for reference.

This form is available to download online at **<familytreeuniversity.com/familykeepsakes>**.

5

Organize for the Future

It's not realistic to think that every family archive will be passed on intact from generation to generation. Sometimes, there are no descendants interested in genealogy or family history, or no descendants at all. Other times, families may decide that the material in their personal possession should be made available to a wider audience.

This chapter will help you decide what to do with items that have social or historical value that could be appreciated by museums and researchers and items that have monetary or sentimental value that could be sold or insured. Two more checkpoints will help you think about the future of your family archive:

Checkpoint 9: Donate Your Family Archive
Checkpoint 10: Plan Your Legacy

DETERMINE HISTORICAL SIGNIFICANCE

Your ancestor or the items he owned may have a greater historical or social significance than you first realize, and a museum or library may be interested in acquiring some of the items you have inherited. The more you know about your ancestor, the better you will be able to determine his place in the community and the potential value of any donations.

I knew my mother-in-law's life was colorful and inspirational, but it took a phone call from a Hawaiian film producer to help me learn another side to her early years as a young woman working in Honolulu. Mary Krantz immigrated from Yugoslavia with her family at age five and went to work in her teens. Moving to Honolulu in the 1930s she found work as a secretary and rubbed elbows with the rich and famous of Hawaii's social set on the weekends. A film producer working on an Oscar-winning documentary of filmmaker Li Ling-Ai came across letters from my mother-in-law in the archives of a Hollywood musical composer. The letters implied that Mary had taken photos and films of the social set that included Ai. The producer wanted to know if I knew of the films. Did they exist and if so, could they be viewed? My answer was yes and yes. There in a scrapbook was Mary with composer Rudolf Friml, Chinese film star Anna May Wong, and filmmaker Li Ling-Ai.

You may not have a connection with the film industry, but do you have an ancestor who served in the Civil War? Correspondence and documents from other men in his regiment or state can help you learn about shared experiences, battles, or other challenges. As time goes by, more and more of these documents have found their way to public archives where they are available to historians and researchers, individuals who realize the value of making historic materials available to a wider audience.

The letters your grandfather wrote home during his military tour of duty are undoubtedly valuable as part of your family history, but they are also significant to historians and researchers as part of the nation's experience during those difficult times. Does this mean that you should donate your entire family archive to a museum? Not necessarily. But, it's something you should definitely consider for the future.

To determine if the personal belongings of your ancestor may hold interest for researchers or historians, begin by asking yourself and other family members a few questions.

Questions to Ask About Your Ancestor

1. Was your ancestor well-known in his career, community, or avocation?
   - Was he active in local government or service organizations?
   - Did he invent a product, start a business, or initiate a new community event or tradition?
   - Was he part of an "ancient" local family?
2. Did he serve in the military?
   - Did he (or she!) have other public service, especially during time of war?
3. Did your ancestor have ties to famous people, events, or places?
   - Was her story ever printed in the newspaper?
   - Did she work for or with a celebrity, business icon, or well-known person or company?
4. Was your ancestor the relative of someone who went on to become famous (or infamous)?
   - How did the person react to fame?
   - What role did your ancestor play in the success, or lack thereof, of his or her relative?

Questions to Ask About the Items

1. For heirlooms objects: Identify the item, place and date of manufacture, condition, and provenance (chain of ownership).
2. For photos: Identify people, places, time, and photographer.
3. For correspondence: Identify writer and recipient, date, and subject of letter.
4. For documents: Identify what it is, persons and places named, dates, and historical significance.

HOW TO DONATE HISTORICAL ITEMS

Remember the Curator's Commandment from chapter one: Do No Harm.

The materials that come into your care may have been lovingly preserved for decades or may crumble into dust at the lightest touch. The best intentions of our parents and grandparents may have caused damage that bring us to tears. Fortunately, we are living in the best of times for archival support and information. Museums, historical societies, libraries, and other repositories are making great efforts to share their knowledge of preservation techniques with the average person. They realize that many items of historical interest and significance have yet to be discovered—they are still tucked away in private family collections.

To a family historian, donating doesn't always mean it's time to call the Salvation Army. Families often choose to donate papers, photographs, or antiques to their local museum or historical society, but few facilities welcome a piano or boxes of photos dropped off at their front door. Most gifts must first be evaluated and approved before acceptance.

Institutions are more likely to be interested in donations when:

- The owner was a significant member of the community, school, or organization, such as mayor, long-time teacher, or club president.
- The item itself is associated with the institution, for example the gavel used by the mayor at the first city council meeting.
- The item is part of a collection that tells a larger story. The gavel, along with a photo of that first city council meeting, and the newspaper account of the event all form a desirable collection.

If you think your item might be of interest to a specific audience, think creatively. Many clubs and organizations welcome contributions to their collections. The city library where your mom volunteered might welcome her area rug for the children's reading room, or be delighted to receive the piano for their community room. Did your uncle work for the railroad? Was your dad a Rotarian? Do a little online research for possible donation sites.

Get creative: If Grandma was a wonderfully ordinary woman who left behind ten boxes of assorted recipes, letters, snapshots, and other paper, consider donating the entire collection to a woman's studies program at your nearby university.

DONATING GENEALOGY RESEARCH

Every genealogy society and library has its own horror stories of the long-time member whose extensive research notes and materials were dropped into a dumpster after the member's demise. Disinterested family members or even jealous spouses have been known to toss out a lifetime of work and valuable resources.

And, truly, sometimes they are hardly to blame. Genealogists who save every scrap of paper, every printout, and every photocopy run the risk of subjecting their heirs to sheer information overload. To the uninitiated, the task of separating original research from mere reference material seems arduous.

If you would like to donate your or someone else's genealogy research, research the acquisition guidelines of the repository you want to donate to by contacting them. Many libraries would prefer not to accept photocopied history books and crumbling newspapers. You may need to do some sorting and organizing prior to donating.

As You Sort Your Archive, Look for and Save:

- original notes
- pedigree charts and family group sheets
- family tree charts
- original source materials

These materials will often be welcomed by local genealogy societies and libraries.

Identify your ancestor's unique interests or talents. Seek out institutions that would like to add your artifacts to their collection. Aim to make your contributions be a "good fit" for the organization's goals. Look beyond your local town library or museum to consider

- regional or national historical societies or museums
- college and university libraries and museums
- state historical societies
- county or city historical societies
- churches, clubs, or schools
- military and organization museums
- occupational museums, such as the Harvey House Museum or Railroad Workers Museums

WHAT'S IT WORTH?

Is it valuable? What a loaded question to ask about an inherited item. *Antiques Roadshow* is only one of many popular television shows built on this exact question: What's it worth? We watch in anticipation of the final gavel, learning along the way about failed restoration, misguided cleaning, and optimistic family legend. Almost every family has a valuable "treasure," but many times the value is based on sentiment rather than actual cash.

TIME: 60 minutes or more

Search the Internet or inquire at your local genealogy society for repositories that may welcome your donation. Expand your search to include regions where your ancestors may have lived or repositories that hold special collections in your area of interest, such as women's studies, westward migration, or ethnic groups.

Find a New Home for Your Materials Step by Step

1. Identify two or three likely places to donate your materials

    Repository: _____

    Contact: _____

    Repository: _____

    Contact: _____

    Repository: _____

    Contact: _____

2. Call or e-mail and ask for a copy of the organization's Mission and Collections Policy.

3. Write down the provenance of your materials (how you came to own the items, see chapter one).

4. Have the items appraised by a certified appraiser, if appropriate.

5. Deliver the materials in good condition. Obtain a receipt for your records.

6. Notify family members where they may find the materials.

This form is available to download online at **<familytreeuniversity.com/familykeepsakes>**.

What is Value?

Value is commonly understood as something's merit, worth, or importance with regards to money, history, culture, art, sentiment, etc. The second half of the definition is often unstated, but it is essential in any evaluation of value.

MONETARY VALUE is the actual market price, the fair purchase price on the open market. Scarcity and condition play a large part in determining monetary value of antiques and artifacts. Collectibles come and go in popularity, and value follows this curve.

HISTORICAL AND CULTURAL VALUE are set by events, people, and places and may or may not carry a corresponding monetary value. Your grandmother's diary may have little monetary value compared to its historical value as a window into the life of a World War I Army nurse. Even so, museums seek out and purchase items for their collections, which helps establish a level of cash value for historical artifacts. The current "black market" in historical and cultural items has created an entire industry based on selling stolen and forged historical artifacts.

ARTISTIC VALUE may demonstrate great skill in painting, sculpture, or other media, but not all "good" art acquires a high monetary value unless the artist, school, or subject matter is already famous. Sometimes, nice paintings are just that—nice, enjoyable paintings of no exceptional monetary or historical value.

SENTIMENTAL VALUE is most familiar to the family historian. Many of us cherish "worthless" little trinkets for the memories they inspire. It isn't uncommon for families to haggle over who gets the cookie jar after Grandma's death. It's not the item, it's the memories that go with it.

INSURANCE

After you have determined that some items may have a special monetary, historical, or artistic value, it's wise to decide if you will continue to keep the items within your family or donate them to an institution. Either way, you should consider having the items appraised by a licensed appraiser.

Be aware that there are different types of appraisals for insurance, estate, and donation purposes. Joe Baratta, appraiser with Abell Auction Company in Los Angeles, says it's important to know what kind of appraisal you need. For insurance purposes, however, an appraisal will take into consideration the cost of replacing the item with one of similar or very similar value. "For one-of-a-kind works, this becomes esoteric," adds Baratta. It's difficult to put a value on a priceless historic artifact.

The term *fair market value* refers to the price that an item would bring on the open market between a willing buyer and a willing seller. This is often different from the intrinsic value that an owner might place on an item. Your grandmother's crystal candy dish may have an intrinsic value within your family of five hundred dollars; that is, you wouldn't consider selling it for less than this amount. Because the dish is old, but not rare, and similar dishes are can be found on eBay in the sixty- to one-hundred dollar price range, an appraisal may determine that the fair market value of the dish is eighty dollars. This may also be the insurance value of the candy dish. If you chose to donate the item, your tax deduction would be eighty dollars.

Estate Appraisal

An estate appraisal will reflect the fair market value and should be close to the amount you might want to take off your income taxes if you donate the item. Families often use the services of an appraiser when settling the estate of a family member who has passed away, whether or not the estate is subject to probate. An appraiser will set a fair market value on items using similar objects that have sold in the marketplace. When multiple heirs are involved in the distribution of personal property, this may be the fairest method to ensure that each party receives the same value from the estate.

Insurance Appraisal

Insurance appraisals focus on setting the "replacement cost" of the item; most standard homeowner's insurance policies do not include fine art, antiques, jewelry, or collectibles. Your insurance company may suggest that you purchase a separate scheduled policy, also known as a "rider" or "floater," for specific items. This is often not as expensive as you might think. Contact your insurance company to determine exactly what you need to do to protect your valuable family heirlooms.

Ask these questions:

1. WHAT DOES YOUR HOMEOWNERS INSURANCE COVER? A standard policy includes coverage for the loss of personal items under the terms of your policy, such as those caused by fire, windstorm, theft, and vandalism. But does your policy cover loss if you drop your grandmother's ring down the sink drain, or damage if your heirloom clock falls to the floor when a nail becomes loose?

2. WHAT IS THE VALUE OF YOUR ITEM? Even without a formal appraisal, you may have a rough guesstimate of the value. Ask your insurance company specifically how you might be compensated for the loss or damage of the item.

3. WHAT IS THE LIMIT OF COVERAGE FOR INDIVIDUAL ITEMS ON YOUR PRESENT POLICY? It may be as low as fifteen hundred dollars for jewelry. Would this cover the cost of your grandfather's pocket watch collection? What is the deductible?

Donation Appraisal

Appraisals for donation purposes are based on the fair market value for the item, that is the price a willing buyer would pay a willing seller in the current market. This appraisal value is useful for a donor who wishes to report the gift as a charitable contribution for income tax purposes.

PLAN TODAY FOR THE FUTURE OF YOUR FAMILY ARCHIVE

Family historians know too well what can happen to a family's treasures from one generation to the next. Photographs of mystery people become separated from larger collections, and the images that might have been identified find their way to thrift store bins and online auctions.

Don't allow your family legacy to be lost. Make provisions for your family history in the same way you include valued items in your estate plan. Identify the items, state your wishes in writing, and let people know your desires. If you foresee that there may be difficulty finding a family member with the interest and ability to care for your family heritage, begin now to investigate places to donate your materials.

Genealogists with research notes and materials need to make the same provisions for their work as they do in finding a home for their family photos and artifacts. A Genealogical Codicil to your Last Will and Testament can provide peace of mind to you and help your beneficiaries decide what to do with your research. A sample Codicil is included in this chapter.

YOUR DIGITAL LIFE

Many genealogists who recognize the difficulty to pass on work between generations are opting to publish their research on the internet. Through blogs, websites, and online services, they post information as they find it, along with scanned images of original source material. If you choose this route, be certain to leave your descendants with whatever they need to access your account after your death. They will need usernames, passwords, and e-mail account access. As more and more of our lives goes online, it is crucial to maintain good records so that your work remains available long after you will no longer access your accounts.

You will use more than one username and password in your digital life. Here are three simple ways to keep track of that information and make it available to your family after you have passed away:

Be Diligent About Recording Passwords

One of the easiest ways to keep track of passwords is to maintain a simple logbook, either on your computer or in a paper notebook. My mother kept a little book next to her computer where she recorded accounts, usernames, e-mail addresses, and passwords. It was a lifesaver when she became ill and we needed access to her accounts to check her utility service and pay bills.

Use a Computer Password Program

Free or inexpensive software programs can keep track of your usernames and passwords and automatically log you into websites you visit. Most of these programs require a Master Password to access other information, so heirs can access all of your information with just one password using your software. See the resources section for a list of popular password manager programs.

Register with a Digital Legacy Service

Online service providers now offer a kind of digital safe deposit box that can hold your personal computer information in trust for a designated beneficiary. This can greatly expedite closing accounts or gaining access in the event of illness or death. Both free and paid services are available from Legacy Locker **<www.legacylocker.com>** and Entrustet **<www.entrustet.com>**.

Checkpoint 10 provides useful tools to plan for the future of your family heirlooms. Use the Genealogical Codicil and the Digital Assets Codicil to specify your wishes. Leave a copy with your estate papers and another with your relatives. Consider leaving a small financial bequest to support any needed archival supplies.

RESOURCES

How to Find a Certified Appraiser

Appraisers Association of America **<www.appraisersassoc.org>**
American Society of Appraisers **<www.appraisers.org>**
Antiquarian Booksellers Association of America **<www.abaa.org>**

Password Managers

LastPass **<www.lastpass.com>**
Roboform (for Windows) **<www.roboform.com>**
1Password (for Mac) **<www.agilebits.com/products/1Password>**
KeePass (cross-platform) **<www. keepass.info>**

Digital Asset Management

Legacy Locker **<www.legacylocker.com>**
Entrustet **<www.entrustet.com>**

TIME: 60 minutes

You Will Need

☐ Genealogical Codicil Form
☐ Digital Assets Codicil Form
☐ folder, binder, or envelope

Plan Your Legacy Step by Step

1. Review the Genealogical Codicil and adapt it to your situation. List possible custodians with contact information for genealogy research and for your family archive. List organizations that may accept donations of your work. Make arrangements with any institutions that you wish to receive your genealogy materials and note this in your codicil.
2. Review the Digital Assets Codicil and adapt it to your situation. Record your e-mail accounts and other membership accounts with password and username.
3. Make copies of both forms and distribute:
   - with your estate papers
   - to your beneficiary, next of kin, or spouse

Checkpoint 10 continued next page

A DIGITAL ASSETS CODICIL TO THE LAST WILL AND TESTAMENT OF

_____

To my spouse, children, guardian, administrator and/or executor:

In the event I am unable to personally access my digital accounts, I do hereby give permission to the persons listed below to use my personal information to gain access to any and all accounts and services in my name, and request that you DO NOT delete any or all of my online information except as indicated below.

In addition, I request that you maintain my genealogy blog or website FOR A PERIOD OF AT LEAST TWO YEARS, during which time you attempt to find a successor to take over this site and maintain the genealogical information posted online. Please contact the persons listed below to see if they would be willing to take on custody of this site or blog.

Funds from my estate in the amount of $_____ are so designated to assist in the cost of this request.

Account	Username	Password	Delete Account (yes or no)	Maintain (duration)
E-mail				
E-mail				
E-mail				
Facebook				
Twitter				
Google				
Pinterest				
Diigo				
Dropbox				
Evernote				
Ancestry.com				

Chart continued next page

Account	Username	Password	Delete Account (yes or no)	Maintain (duration)
Blog				
Website				
Format				

Signature _____ Date _____

List of potential digital custodians here

_____ phone/e-mail: _____

_____ phone/e-mail: _____

_____ phone/e-mail: _____

This form is available to download online at **<familytreeuniversity.com/familykeepsakes>**.

A GENEALOGICAL CODICIL TO THE LAST WILL AND TESTAMENT OF

_____

To my spouse, children, guardian, administrator and/or executor:

Upon my demise, I do hereby request that you DO NOT dispose of any or all of my research and genealogical materials, prepared personally by me or those prepared by others which may be in my possession, including but not limited to books, files, notebooks, digital files, computer programs, or materials stored in my family archive, known also as _____ _____ FOR A PERIOD OF TWO YEARS.

During this time period, please attempt to find one or more persons who would be willing to take custody of the said materials and the responsibility of maintaining and continuing the family histories and research. Please contact the persons listed below to inquire if they would be willing to take on the custody of these items.

I do not wish to place an undue burden on the executors of my estate; therefore, in the event you are unable to find someone to accept these materials, please contact a historical or genealogical organization that I have been a member of to determine if they will accept some parts or all of my materials. (List of organizations and addresses below.)

It is my desire that you honor this wish to preserve my genealogical and historical research endeavors and pass them on to future generations.

Signature _____   Date _____

Witness _____   Date _____

Witness _____   Date _____

List of potential custodians here

_____   phone/e-mail: _____

_____   phone/e-mail: _____

_____   phone/e-mail: _____

List of organizations here

_____   contact: _____

_____   contact: _____

_____   contact: _____

Access information for my digital files is located _____

This Codicil is adapted from many found on Internet forums and websites.

This form is available to download online at <**familytreeuniversity.com/familykeepsakes**>.

6

Organize Archival Papers

N ow that you are ready to move your family treasures into archival storage, take time to review best practices for preserving the items in your archive. This section contains information on Organizing Options and Storage Solutions for specific heirloom items. You will also find specific Cautions and Tips for working with the materials. This chapter covers paper-based items; chapter seven discusses photographs and film, and chapter eight deals with artifacts and collectibles.

Resources in this chapter include archival suppliers and where to find more information about proper preservation of artifacts and memorabilia.

THE PAPER TIGER

Receipts. Newspaper clippings. Old letters. Scrapbooks. Address books. All have one thing in common—all are made from paper, in its many colors, shapes, and sizes. And while nineteenth-century letters may have been scripted on fine rag paper, close contact with a scrap of yellowed newspaper can cause permanent stain and damage.

If your inherited archive is free from paper trash, consider yourself lucky. I have worked with dozens of family collections and over half held from moderate to extreme quantities of paper trash. Why? Because paper is free or cheap, it comes to you, it has many worthwhile uses, and, for many people, it's hard to resist.

All that paper can be too much for some people. Saving vital information is one thing, saving an entire lifetime of cancelled checks is quite another. As curators, we might have just a teeny-bit of hoarder in our own DNA. Be strong. You don't want to end up on reality television with your closets and cabinets thrown open to the world. When it comes to paper, you can feel just fine about throwing away quite a bit.

There's saving, and then, there's saving. Whatever bits of paper you do decide to keep, it helps to know the full cost of your decision.

The Cost of Archiving Your Stuff

As you begin to sort and organize your archive, ask yourself: Is this item worth the time and the cost of archival supplies to be processed for your archive? Maybe the item is not vital, but nonetheless, is interesting. I suggest you consider a three-part evaluation of materials. Instead of saving everything, decide if something is:

1. VITAL: The paper gives lineage information or other key information about the person, place, or event, or it confirms or refutes family tradition. Handle these items with care and conservation. Digitize the image, store the original, and index file names and descriptions.

2. NOT VITAL, ADDS COLOR: This paper adds color and interesting information about the person, place, or event. You have several options when deciding what to do with nonvital items. You can leave the items in the original box, or move all similar items to one community archival box. Maintain a General Index on the Inventory Sheet. Digitize as needed. If the information on the paper is more useful than the actual piece of paper, consider making a digital copy and discarding the paper. Or place the item in less optimal storage.

3. NOT ARCHIVAL: If a paper doesn't add personal information, don't bother saving it as part of your family archive. If the information is of interest to only you, keep it somewhere outside of the archive. For example, if you enjoy scrapbooking or crafting, move interesting bits of ephemera to your scrapbooking supplies. I have a small plastic shoebox filled with 1950s valentines, sweet bookmarks, and other bits of the past that I enjoy using in collage and handmade greeting cards.

Review all the items in your archive box by box, and consider giving your full attention and resources to only those items that really count. When you are tempted to save odd bits of cool ephemera, remember your original goal to preserve your family history. Take care of the vital stuff first.

CORRESPONDENCE

Family letters are among the most valuable heirlooms in any archive. Correspondence can provide new information or verify family legends about births, deaths, and marriages. Historians love family letters for the rich details they reveal about relationships and everyday life. Reading old letters can become almost addicting; it's hard to stop mid-story. All that handling can damage old paper. Envelopes become brittle, and folded stationery can crack and break along the crease.

Use the original order of groups and packets to help identify mystery letters. Whenever you encounter a group of letters bundled or tied together, make a note of all the letters in the group and indicate what held them together (e.g., tied together with blue ribbon or inside a larger envelope).

Organizing Options

1. Organize chronologically, by date sent. (Use the postmark or date on the letter whenever possible.)
2. Organize by recipient.
3. Organize by sender. (Note: the author is the recognized copyright owner of the letter.)
4. Organize by kind of correspondence: family, business, church, etc.

Storage Solutions

- Remove letters from envelopes, unfold and place the letter and envelope together in an archival folder or paper sleeve.
- For large correspondence collections, place several paper sleeves inside one archival folder.
- Label the sleeve or folder with the date, sender, and recipient.
- Store sleeves or folders either in archival flat boxes or vertical file boxes.
- Hanging file folders are also an option for document storage. Archival-quality hanging folders are preferred, but regular office folders can be used as long as the documents are first placed inside archival-quality file folders. Use your best judgment with extremely old or important documents.

Cautions

- Keep items of the same size together as much as possible.
- If a folded document is brittle, leave as is, do not force it open.
- Remove staples, paper clips, wire or other metal. (See the Safely Remove Staples sidebar in this chapter.)
- Remove and discard twine or rubber bands.
- Always store letters and envelopes together.
- Store no more than ten to fifteen sheets in the same folder.
- Isolate any newsprint enclosures; scan or photocopy to rag paper and include with original.
- To protect the paper, avoid folding and refolding letters. Leave them opened flat.
- Remember to note any groups or packets of letters.

Tips

Working with letters is a time-consuming task. Break the task it into steps, if necessary. Proceed through each step as you have time.

1. Move the letters to archival sleeves and folders.
2. Scan, if desired, read, and label (see chapters nine and ten).
3. Transcribe or extract, preferably using digitized images.

It's very important for letters to be stored flat in archival sleeves. Do this first and then, when you have time to add file names and read or transcribe the letters, they can be handled more easily and with less damage from folding and refolding.

NEWSPAPERS AND CLIPPINGS

Newsprint is so damaging to other items that many museums will no longer accept clippings or newspapers in an archival donation. Archivists also encourage digitizing and printing a copy on archival-quality paper, instead of saving the original. Watch for poor-quality paper and isolate it from other materials.

I have several original newspapers from the early twentieth century that feature dramatic news articles about my grandmother and her first husband. Although preserving the information in the articles is my first priority, I also want to preserve the newspaper itself.

Full-size newspapers are too large to be safely or accurately scanned on a standard 8.5" × 11" personal scanner, but that doesn't mean you can't create a digital copy of them. Instead of scanning, use digital photography to capture the image. Lay your newspaper flat on the floor and stand above the paper to photograph it with a digital camera. Use natural light and turn off the flash. You should be able to snap a good quality image that will be readable on your computer screen.

After scanning clippings or photographing full sheets, I print copies on archival-grade paper and write the newspaper name, date, and page number on the copy. The photocopy is stored with other original documents because the actual newsprint would damage the other papers in the box. I place the original newspaper flat for storage in a large archival box with other newspapers and clippings.

Organizing Options

Keep all original newspapers and clippings together and stored separately from other materials. Organize copies of clippings with other original documents to suit your objectives:

1. Organize by subject (obituaries, wedding notices, etc.).
2. Organize by person.
3. Organize chronologically.

Storage Solutions

- Scan clippings; print them out on archival paper and store the new printout with other documents in archival storage. Discard the originals, if you wish.
- If you must save the newspaper original, place clippings in an archival plastic folder or sleeve supported by a sheet of buffered archival paper, and group pages inside an archival folder. Store flat with full-size newspapers or in separate box or folder of clippings.

Cautions

- Add citation information to printouts of clippings; handwrite with archival pen or pencil.
- Modern newspaper and newsprint will destroy anything it touches. Isolate it from all other materials.
- Laminating was a popular newspaper "preservation" method in the mid-1900s, but both the plastic laminate and the pulp paper are nonarchival. If you keep old laminated clippings, store them separately from other materials.
- For many years deacidification sprays and homemade solutions were suggested to preserve newsprint. The Northeast Document Conservation Center no longer recommends this method for preserving newspapers, and instead encourages printing scanned images on archival-quality paper.

Tips

- Place all your newsprint in one file. Then set aside a block of time to scan or photograph the entire collection. If you can't do it all at once, work in batches.
- Handle newspapers and newsprint materials as little as possible, work from scanned images for transcribing.

DOCUMENTS

Marriage certificates, property deeds, school diplomas, and legal documents are often printed or handwritten on high-quality paper and survive for centuries in excellent condition. These may include vital documents, so do all you can to preserve them properly.

Other paper documents, such as receipts, lists, and notes don't fare so well, mostly because they were printed or written on inexpensive, poor-quality paper. The information likely wasn't meant to be kept for a long time.

Always isolate anything made of newsprint or cheap-grade paper. It's not worth damaging your grandfather's Last Will and Testament by stacking it with a crumbling cleaning receipt. Just because a loved one kept the paper, doesn't mean you have to. Remember to identify papers as vital or nonvital, and keep nonvital items only if you feel they really contribute value to your archive.

Organizing Options

1. Organize by person.
2. Organize by size.
3. Organize by kind of item: vital records, property, school, etc.

Storage Solutions

- Store items of the same size together, flat, or upright supported in archival-quality folders.
- Place folders in archival boxes or in hanging file folders in a filing cabinet.

Cautions

- Remove staples, paper clips, wire, or other metal. (See the sidebar on special techniques for removing safely.)
- Remove twine or rubber bands and discard.
- Unfold documents and store flat.
- If a folded document is brittle, leave as is, do not force open.
- Isolate any newsprint enclosures, scan or photocopy to rag paper, and include with original documents in your storage of choice.

Safely Remove Staples

Carefully remove any of the following you find attached to documents or lying loose in your family archive:

- metal staples
- wire
- hairpins
- paper clips
- fasteners

Old staples can present a particular challenge. Don't use a modern staple remover; this may tear or crease the old document. Follow these steps instead.

1. Slide a piece of thin, stiff plastic under the staple on both sides of the paper (an old credit card cut into strips works well for this). The plastic helps cushion the paper from the stress of removing the staple.
2. Bend up the open ends of the staple and pull it free from the paper. Use tweezers or a thin knife if necessary.
3. Discard the staple. Store the pages of the document together in an archival folder.

SCRAPBOOKS, BABY ALBUMS, AND EPHEMERA

Scrapbooks and handmade albums, by their very nature, are filled with a mix of materials—a carefully pressed flower, a crumbling receipt for a prom dress, baby's wrist band from the hospital. These items may have 3-D surfaces that are attached to the page with glue, ribbon, or metal. They also may include botanical or once-living specimens. That's what makes them so wonderful! Ephemeral best describes the contents of many scrapbooks and baby albums. They are filled with items that were never intended to last for posterity.

Consider creating a digital copy of the album to refer to in your family history research, allowing the original to be stored undisturbed. High-quality scanned images can also be used to create a reproduction edition that can be shared with family and friends as a printed book or in e-book format.

Your archive may be a sort of scrapbook in itself. I've seen archives that included recipe cards, old-fashioned postcards, valentines, vintage greeting cards, and knitting patterns. Most of these materials can be cared for in the same way as documents and papers.

Organizing Options

1. Organize by size and kind: postcards, greeting cards, recipes, etc.
2. Organize by decade or era.
3. Keep assorted items together as a sort of time capsule.

Storage Solutions

- Because scrapbooks may be filled with toxic nonarchival elements, it's important to store them separately from other items to avoid cross-contamination. Using archival boxes for your albums and scrapbooks can help preserve them as long as possible by not contributing to further damage.
- Place items of same size and kind in an appropriate-sized archival box.
- Make or buy an archival folder to enclose scrapbooks or albums, and then place them inside a similar-sized archival box to hold multiple books.
- You may want to consider conservation of significant scrapbooks or albums by disassembling the album and encasing individual pages in archival plastic. Refer to the Northeast Document Conservation Center for more information.

Cautions

- Remove or isolate any caustic materials.
- Use buffered tissue paper to cushion scrapbook edges within the box.

Tips

- Remember to transcribe or abstract any genealogically important information from the pages of albums and scrapbooks and the back sides of postcards.
- Photograph or scan each page of the album to create a "digital album" record copy in case the original deteriorates.
- Scan ephemera to use in your own digital scrapbooks and creative projects.
- Take photographs of the album and assorted items to use as memory joggers when looking for new ideas for your own family history projects.

JOURNALS, DIARIES, FAMILY BIBLES

Conservators recommend that bound books be stored upright on shelving; however, handwritten volumes, such as journals and diaries, and unique books, such as a family Bible, should be handled individually as bound manuscripts and stored in archival book boxes or four-flap enclosures.

Organizing Options

1. Organize by author or subject.
2. Organize chronologically.

Storage Solutions

- Enclose fragile books in handmade or purchased archival four-flap folders.
- Place diaries, journals, and Bibles individually in drop spine boxes and store flat on shelving.

Cautions

- Remove bookmarks and pressed flowers from pages of books.
- Do not stack books flat more than two or three volumes high.
- Avoid writing in the book itself. Add identifying notes to the box or folder.

Tips

- Look for book and pamphlet storage options in archival catalogs.
- 100 percent cotton tape may be used to hold loose pages together.

YEARBOOKS AND PRINTED BOOKS

Most family collections include a few books—high school and college yearbooks, favorite cookbooks, novels, or poetry volumes. Conservators recommend that stable bound books be stored upright on shelving unless they are rare or in poor condition.

For most of us, the best and easiest place to store family books is right in with our current volumes. Your bookcase is probably located in the temperate environment of your family room, living room, or den and relatively free from dust, insects, and extreme fluctuations in temperature or humidity.

Organizing Options

1. Organize by subject.
2. Organize by owner if you are caring for the archives of several ancestors.

Storage Solutions

- Store printed books, such as yearbooks, upright in your archival storage location.
- Store printed books in a designated location on your home bookshelves. Keep a list in your archive so you remember where they are.
- Store damaged or fragile books flat inside archival folders or closed boxes.

Cautions

- Remove bookmarks and pressed flowers from pages of books.
- Take care when removing upright books from shelves. Do not pull the volume by the spine; instead push back on the volumes on either side and grasp the volume to remove.
- Avoid writing in the book itself. Add identifying notes on a piece of archival paper inserted in the front of the book.
- Use a hose attachment to vacuum your bookshelves regularly to keep them dust-free.

Tips

- Look for book and pamphlet storage options in archival catalogs.
- Protect the cover or dust jacket with clear archival plastic covers.

GENEALOGY RESEARCH MATERIALS

Are you a second- or third-generation genealogist? Does research run in your genes? Does your family archive include boxes of genealogy research, printed pedigree charts, handwritten family group sheets, and carefully photocopied source material?

When my sister and I inherited our mom's stuff, we had no idea that Mom was such a good record keeper. She must have heard the "Cite Your Sources" chorus because her files were filled with photocopied pages from books, Web printouts, and copied correspondence. It's a genealogist's dream to find source material right there with the research, but what do you do when the sheer volume of material threatens to take over your own home or your own research materials?

First, go back and look at your goals in accepting the responsibility of your family archive. Do you want to extend your pedigree? Or are you working on a family history book? Whatever your goal, you owe it to yourself to screen the new materials with an eye for moving forward. You do not have to be overwhelmed and burdened by someone else's stuff.

Take a page from the archivists at the New England Historic Genealogical Society. Archivist Judy Lucey works with donors to select materials for the society archives. She avoids adding photocopies of available journals and research materials. This is duplicated material you can find somewhere, so there's no need to keep it. She also declines original newspapers because they contain acid that can damage other items they are stored with. Feel free to apply these two principles to your archive and get rid of material guilt-free. If you want to keep newspapers, follow the storage and preservation advice outlined earlier in this chapter.

In vetting Mom's genealogy research, I moved her original notes to a new plastic file box, eliminating any duplicated material I found.

I SAVED
- Mom's handwritten notes
- e-mail printouts and copies of correspondence
- books, articles, magazines I wanted to read

I DIDN'T SAVE

- genealogy society journals (donated to my local society)
- duplicates of census records and other sources I already had in my own research
- books I owned (I donated these)
- pedigree charts and family group sheets that duplicated my own information and research
- copies of stuff I had sent Mom

I MADE DIGITAL COPIES AND DISCARDED THE PAPER ORIGINALS FOR: some research material from unknown sources; I didn't want to lose the material, but it was more than one hundred pages, and I didn't want to store it. My ScanSnap sheet-fed scanner made quick work of the pile.

Organizing Options

1. Organize research by creator. Order a custom rubber stamp with the researcher's name to identify his or her work.
2. Organize by family line. Identify work from other researchers.

Storage Solutions

- Keep these material separate from your own work in a designated file space.
- Store paper files in plastic file bins. This is not archival storage.
- Store historic documents in archival storage following the appropriate guidelines in this chapter.

Cautions

- Keep pages together. Unless you are handling historic documents, use paper clips and staples as needed.
- Remember your own goals; your inherited research should be a blessing, not a burden.

Tips

- Discard duplicate copies of the material.
- If you are overwhelmed, frustrated, or just strapped for space, consider scanning your inherited research files. Office copy services will do this at a reasonable cost.
- Consider investing in OCR software that can create searchable full-text documents.

RESOURCES

Preserving Documents

National Archives **<www.archives.gov/preservation/family-archives>**

Northeast Document Conservation Center **<www.nedcc.org/resources/resources.php>**

7

Organize Archival Photos

Documents may share the everyday details of our ancestor's lives, but photographs allow us to see firsthand the same high brow or broad smile we inherited from our grandparent and admire jewelry or artifacts that we now own. This chapter will focus on caring for the photographs and film that you find in your family archive.

Resources will direct you to archival suppliers and photo experts to help you identify the kinds of photos in your collection and where to learn more about them.

PHOTOS, PHOTOS, EVERYWHERE

As you work with your family archive, be prepared to find photographs and film anywhere and everywhere. When emptying my aunt's home to prepare it for sale, we didn't want to take time to go through the contents of all her closets and drawers. A brief look showed that, over the years, important documents and photos had been layered with household receipts and advertising brochures. I transferred individual drawers to boxes and brought the contents home to examine more closely. The first box I sorted showed me that this had been a wise decision. Mixed in with free note pads from the local Realtor I found two antique cabinet card photographs of my grandmother taken when she was an infant and toddler. These treasures could have been lost forever; look carefully before tossing the trash.

I've found old photos inside books, tucked in letters, curled inside a vase, tacked to the back of a picture frame, and underneath dresser drawer paper lining. Wallet-sized photos might be in wallets or purses, and tiny photos were often trimmed for jewelry. Cased photographs, like tintypes and daguerreotypes, might be mixed in with books or other artifacts. Look everywhere and bring the photos you find to one place where you can sort and arrange for storage.

When working with photographs and films, always have clean hands, and wear cotton gloves when handling film or fragile photos. Specific precautions for each photography type are detailed in this chapter. In general, take the following precautions when handling any type of photography:

- Wear white cotton gloves when handling antique photographs or film, or wash your hands.
- Do not touch the surface of the image.
- Hold images by the edges.
- Avoid light and heat near photos and film.
- Store photos and film in a moderate temperature; avoid extremes.
- Use only archival storage materials that pass the PAT test.
- Use compressed air to gently remove any dust.
- Do not write directly on the image. Use only a soft lead pencil for notes on the reverse side. Better yet, make any notes on a paper sleeve.

ANTIQUE PHOTOGRAPHS

Ambrotypes, tintypes, daguerreotypes, cabinet cards, carte de visite, stereo vision cards. The world of antique photography includes a variety of methods, processes, sizes, and materials. Understanding the process used to create the images in your collection can help you identify mystery photographs and potentially extend your family tree. If you find antique images in your collection, take time to learn exactly what you have so that you can properly care for your treasures.

Photo experts Maureen Taylor, The Photo Detective, and scientist Colleen Fitzpatrick are helpful resources for genealogists who inherit family history photos, and give frequent lectures and seminars. Photo collector footnoteMaven publishes an online magazine, *Shades of the Departed Magazine*, filled with informative articles about the world of antique photos. Photo restorer and collector Gary Clark shares his knowledge in a helpful website and e-book. See the Resources section of this chapter for links.

EARLY CASED IMAGES

EXAMPLES: Daguerreotypes, Ambrotypes, Tintypes

The earliest photographs date from 1839 when Louis Daguerre popularized an accessible, affordable, and astounding new invention—the daguerreotype. Our ancestors surely thought they were living in the "modern age" when a photographic portrait could be produced economically in a relatively short amount of time. The first photographs were made directly onto a rigid glass or metal plate that was sealed in a glass-front case for protection and framing. Portraits were no longer only for the rich. For the first time in history, the average person could have his or her likeness recorded to be viewed by contemporary family and friends and future generations.

The small size and easy portability of early cased photographs were among their most popular features, but also contributed to their damage and scarcity today. Unlike oil portraits that remained hanging in a family home for generations, cased images were easily lost, damaged, or misplaced among other items. Few images include any kind of identification and, when the photo is separated from the owner or family, it can be difficult to identify the subject.

Daguerreotypes, ambrotypes, and tintypes are all examples of early cased images, but the processes used to create these three types of photos are different. Here's how to distinguish between the three.

DAGUERREOTYPES. These were the first photographs. They are positive images on copper plates and usually encased between glass and a mat. The image is only visible when the photo is seen from an angle.

TINTYPES. These are similar to daguerreotypes, but made on polished iron plates, and are visible when viewed straight-on. (Hint: Hold a small magnet to the back of the plate—an iron tintype will attract the magnet, the copper daguerreotype will not.)

AMBROTYPES. These are negative images on glass plates (meaning the image is flipped) but appears positive due to a dark backing. The image is reflective but can be viewed from all angles. The glass plate is not magnetic.

Caring for Cased Images

Don't worry if you have difficulty determining whether your photos are daguerreotypes, tintypes, or ambrotypes. The care for antique cased images is the same. Photographs should be stored in close-fitting individual archival folders inside an archival box. It is important that both the folder enclosures and the box fit the photo snugly to prevent damage from sliding and scratching.

Cased images are easily damaged. Seek out a professional conservator if your images need repair or restoration.

Organizing Options

1. Organize antique images by kind and size.
2. Organize by family or archive.

Storage Solutions

- Place individual images in a custom-made or purchased four-flap enclosure.
- Store in individual archival boxes.
- Store in a cool (but not cold) and dry environment.

Cautions

- Do not place daguerreotypes in cold storage.
- Do not try to reframe or force into new cases.
- Consult a conservator for restoration or repair. Do not attempt this yourself.
- Cased images have become highly collectible. Consider insuring your images if you have a large collection.

BLACK-AND-WHITE PHOTOGRAPHS

Within a few decades of its invention, photography had progressed to include the innovation of albumen prints made from a glass negative on paper coated with an egg white mixture. The resulting print was typically mounted on card stock of varying sizes, the most popular being the small calling-card sized carte de visite (visiting card), which was 2½" × 4", and the mid-size cabinet card, which was 4¼" × 6½".

The card mounting stock provided an added benefit for the photographer; he now had a ready spot for his imprint and advertising. Today, antique photo collectors use information about the photographers, card stock, image size, and shape to help identify the date and location of the photo subject.

Fast forward to the twentieth century and the world of personal photography. My grandmother was a real shutterbug. Her letters refer to using her Kodak Brownie camera on outings, and the hundreds of black-and-white snapshots and negatives she created attest to her fascination with photography. My sons must have inherited her flair for light and setting because our own albums are filled with their efforts to capture life on film.

The enduring popularity of black-and-white photography must be at least partly due to its reputation as a long-lasting photographic medium. Well-processed negatives and prints will survive decades with reasonable care, yielding images that are as crisp and bright today as when they were first printed.

Organizing Options

1. Organize by subject, event, family, or place, depending on your purpose.
2. Organize by size.
3. Organize by photographer.
4. For large collections, do not sort by person, subject, or event. Instead sort by type and size, and assign each individual image a file number marked on the archival sleeve.
5. Organize and display in an archival photo album.

Storage Solutions

- Store prints in archival-grade paper or clear plastic sleeves or envelopes.
- Store same-sized prints together, stacking carefully to avoid scratching. Place rare prints in individual sleeves.
- Store envelopes vertically in same-sized archival boxes.

Cautions

- Do not write directly on images. Make any notes on a paper sleeve. Avoid light, which causes images to fade.
- Avoid extreme heat or cold; these temperatures cause prints to become dry and brittle.
- Avoid humidity and damp conditions to prevent curling and warping.
- Avoid stacking prints of varying sizes because movement within the stacks can cause scratches or tears.
- Make digital copies for display or scrapbooking.
- Do not use a magnetic photo album.

Tips

- Scan images in batches.
- Work with one size print at a time.

STEREOGRAPHS

My grandparents had exactly three diversions available for visiting children: a wooden stacking game called Blockhead, a set of wooden pick-up-sticks, and a wicker basket filled with old stereo-scope cards and a wooden viewer. My younger sister and I played the games for a short time and, eventually, I was left alone with the basket of old photographs. One by one I viewed the marvels of the nation's natural wonders—the Grand Canyon, Niagara Falls, Yellowstone's Old Faithful.

Stereograph photos are actually two separate images printed side by side. The viewer causes your eyes to see the same images independent of each other. Viewing the images this way causes your brain to process the two single photos as a three-dimensional image.

The earliest stereo views were produced as daguerreotypes, glass, or porcelain images. Ste-reoscope photos were produced on card stock as late as 1938. The stereoscope cards I viewed as a child in the 1950s and 60s were probably created before the 1920s.

Organize and store your stereoscope cards following the guidelines for the materials they are made from. Rigid images on metal, glass, or porcelain should be cared for following preserva-tion techniques for cased images; stereoscope cards should be preserved like early paper prints.

Organizing Options

1. Organize by theme or subject.
2. Organize by decade.
3. Organize by type of image and size: glass, card stock, etc.

Storage Solutions

- Store in clear sleeves for protection.
- File individual stereoscope cards in a specialty archival box.

Cautions

- Handle carefully when viewing in a stereoscope viewer.

Optimal Storage Conditions

The best conditions for preventing deterioration of your black-and-white photograph collection are:

A temperature around 68°F

Relative humidity level of 30–40 percent

According to the Library of Congress, black-and-white photos are "easiest to maintain in an interior closet or air-conditioned room—not in an attic or basement."

Tips

- Add "new" cards to your collection from online auctions and ephemera dealers.
- Stereoscope cards are a great introduction to family history for children.
- Learn more about stereograph images at the American Antiquarian Society in Worcester, Massachusetts **<www.americanantiquarian.org/stereographs.htm>**.

COLOR PHOTOGRAPHS

We've become so accustomed to the bright, high-definition colors of digital photography that it's sometimes hard to remember that amateur color photography is not yet one hundred years old. Eastman Kodak's revolutionary color negative film and affordable Kodak cameras brought color photography into millions of homes and backyards in the 1930s. The new technology allowed families to compare shades of orange and red hair between cousins, even when they lived in distant cities.

Color photos are especially prone to fading when exposed to light, but even images stored in the dark may be susceptible to color shift and a yellowish haze caused by the dye used in the original film. Fortunately, scanning and digital restoration can bring back much of the original color in old prints. Look for scanning companies that offer this service, or investigate the "Auto Restore" options of your personal scanner.

Organizing Options

1. Organize by subject, place, or event.
2. Organize chronologically.

Storage Solutions

- Store prints in archival paper or plastic sleeves.
- Store in a cool place, 40ºF or less.
- Store in a dry environment, about 30 percent humidity.

Cautions

- The cooler your keep your photos, the longer they will last; however, be wary of refrigerating prints or film as the humidity can cause other problems.
- Make digital copies for display or scrapbooking.
- Do not use a magnetic photo album.

Tips

- Scan images in batches.
- Work with one size print at a time.

SLIDES

Did you inherit an avalanche of slide carousels and little yellow boxes of mounted slides? The relatively inexpensive cost of Kodachrome slides is both its best and worst feature. Photographers felt the freedom to take countless photos—a blessing to shutterbugs. But too often, they didn't dispose of "rejects," leaving their descendants with boxes and trays of nearly identical images.

Your first order of business may be to rent or borrow a slide projector and quickly triage the images left in your care. Discard duplicates and damaged images guilt-free. My uncle's slide collection was demoted to the garage for many years, and now I expect to find very few images worth saving in those carousels.

Color slides, like film and negatives, can be preserved almost indefinitely when placed in cold storage. Most home archives don't have freezer space to devote to archival storage, but if you do, seek out specialized information on preparing film for cold storage to avoid the pitfalls of cold temperatures and fluctuating humidity. See the resources at the end of this chapter for more information.

Organizing Options

1. Organize by subject, place, or event.
2. Organize chronologically.
3. Organize by photographer.

Storage Solutions

- Store vertically in archival boxes in your home archive.

Caution

- Items placed in cold storage are susceptible to moisture if brought to room temperature quickly. See the Resources section for specialized cold storage references.

Tips

- Instead of viewing slides on a projector, locate a portable slide viewer. I found a great one for twenty dollars at a local thrift store that displays the image on a 9" white plastic screen. This small size is fine for deciding which images to save and which to throw away.
- When inserting slides into plastic sleeves, be careful not to bend or force the slides.
- A binder box is a good choice for slide storage; it provides a binder for plastic slide pages and closes like a box to protect the pages from dust and light.

NEGATIVES

I thought I had already seen all the photos in my grandmother's collection until I stumbled upon a yellow paper packet crammed with old black-and-white negatives. Measuring a generous 2¾" × 4¼", the negatives contained images I had never seen before—mostly young, handsome soldiers first hamming it up with a few pretty girls, and then looking seriously at the lens as they struck a regimental pose. It was a moment in time captured on film.

Don't overlook the negatives in your collection or assume that prints were made and still exist. Unless damaged, negatives will yield fresh crisp prints for archiving with better results than scanning a print of the same image.

Before organizing, scanning, or storing your negatives, be certain that you are working with safety film. Review the sidebar about cellulose nitrate and cellulose acetate films. These films are highly toxic and dangerous.

Organizing Options

1. Organize by subject, place, or event.
2. Organize chronologically.
3. Organize by photographer.

Storage Solutions

- Store in paper or plastic archival negative sleeves in archival boxes in your home archive.
- Store in a binder box; it provides a binder for plastic pages that closes like a box to protect the pages from dust and light.
- Keep negatives a in cool location.

The Dangers of Cellulose Nitrate and Acetate Film

When you find old negatives, film, or slides in your collection, first determine if the film is safe before proceeding. Black-and-white negatives and early movie film may have also been made of cellulose nitrate, a highly explosive product. "Bursting into flames" is a real possibility when cellulose nitrate film is part of your collection.

Improved "safety film" made of cellulose acetate aimed to provide a more stable medium, but proved to be subject to "Vinegar Syndrome." As the film degraded, it turned into acetic acid, or vinegar. You can often detect cellulose acetate negatives or movie film from the vinegar odor. If you notice a peculiar sour vinegar odor in your negatives or film, remove the offender immediately before it causes damage to other items in your collection. Plan to copy or digitize as soon as possible.

Around 1960, film was made out of polyester, which has proven to be both safe and stable. But you will want to immediately remove from your collection any negatives and movie film that you suspect may be cellulose nitrate or cellulose acetate. Smithsonian preservationist Don Williams recommends using the following test to determine the kind of film in your collection.

Test Your Film

You will need two pairs of Polaroid sunglasses.

1. Lay the two pair of sunglasses one on top of the other and rotate the top pair 90 degrees so the glasses are perpendicular to each other.
2. Insert the negative or filmstrip between the two pairs of glasses.
3. Shine a bright light over the top lens so it goes through the top lens, film, and bottom lens.
4. If you see a darkened light with no rainbows, the film is either cellulose nitrate or cellulose acetate. Both are potentially harmful and dangerous and will need to be disposed of.
5. If you see rainbows, the film is polyester. It is stable and safe to keep.

What to Do With Dangerous Film

If you encounter cellulose nitrate and cellulose acetate film, remove it immediately from your collection. Store in a cool place and plan to digitize or copy as soon as possible. Don't keep the film in a freezer used for food storage because it builds up toxic substances.

Contact your local library or museum for information about digitizing images. Do *not* discard films into your regular trash. Cellulose nitrate film is considered hazardous waste and must be disposed of properly. Contact your local waste disposal office for more information.

Cautions

- Make sure you are working with safety film; if your negatives are cellulose nitrate and cellulose acetate, plan to copy the images and destroy the negatives as soon as possible.

Tips

- Scan negatives using a special negative holder that holds the film along the edges to prevent contact with the glass bed of the scanner.
- Negatives and slides should be scanned at higher resolution than prints. See chapter nine for details.

FILM AND VIDEO

We needed a 16mm projector to view movies my mother-in-law made when she lived in Hawaii in the 1930s. I found a likely looking Bell & Howell model on craigslist and drove across town to meet the seller. He was keen on adding a few items to our bill, including some vintage movie reels still in their board and metal boxes. He pulled back the straps and we nearly passed out from the strong odor of vinegar that rolled out of the box. The film was surely cellulose acetate degrading with a full case of "Vinegar Syndrome." If you encounter this in your archive, follow the steps outlined in The Dangers of Cellulous Nitrate and Acetate Film sidebar.

Organizing Options

1. Organize film and videos chronologically and by subject.
2. Organize by type of film: 8mm, 16mm, cassette, etc.

Storage Solutions

- Store vertically in archival boxes in your home archive.
- Film, like negatives and slides, is best preserved in cold temperatures. Store in a cool location.
- Digitize for preservation; see chapter nine for options.

Caution

- Items placed in cold storage are susceptible to moisture if brought to room temperature quickly. See the Resources section for specialized cold storage references.

Tips

- Look for local professional film storage if you want to store old films in optimal conditions.

RESOURCES

Identifying Old Family Photographs

Gary Clark, PhotoTree **<www.PhotoTree.com>**

Colleen Fitzpatrick, PhD, Forensic Genealogist **<www.forensicgenealogy.info>**

footnoteMaven **<www.ShadesoftheDeparted.com>**

Maureen Taylor, The Photo Detective **<www.maureentaylor.com>**

STORING PHOTOGRAPHS AND FILM

The Association of Moving Image Archivists, Film Forever Home Film Preservation Guide **<www.filmforever.org>**

Library of Congress, Care, Handling and Storage of Motion Picture Film **<www.loc.gov/preservation/care/film.html>**

Little Film, Home Movies: A Basic Primer **<littlefilm.org/Primer.html>**

National Archives, Cold Storage Handling Guidelines for Photographs **<www.archives.gov/preservation/storage/cold-storage-photos.html>**

8

Organize Artifacts

Artifacts aren't limited to objects excavated on an archeological dig. Your great-grandfather's pocket watch and your aunt's Depression-era quilt are good examples of the kind of objects you might find in your family archive. Curators and collectors use the term *artifact* for the many man-made objects that acquire historical or artistic significance. For the family historian, artifacts may assume emotional and sentimental value as well.

Preserving inherited artifacts isn't necessarily complicated, especially if the object is on display or used in your home. Some items need a bit of extra TLC (tender loving care), but most objects likely will be just fine with the same care and attention you give everything else in your home. If you will be storing artifacts, you will need to take the standard precautions against extreme temperatures, moisture, and pests.

This chapter highlights artifacts often found in a family archive and offers practical suggestions for caring for your heirlooms. The resources at the end of this chapter will help you find archival supplies and information for specialized situations.

ART

Consider yourself most fortunate if you inherited portraits, paintings, or other fine art in your family archive. Your treasures may portray your ancestor's likeness in paint, chalk, or ink, or they may demonstrate the skill of a family artist.

Care

- If you have your artwork framed, use only archival-quality materials.
- Use recommended framing procedures. For example, oil paintings should be framed without glass; watercolors, prints, and photographs should be secured behind archival mats and then framed with UV-filter glass. Refer to the Resources section for more information.
- The American Institute for Conservation of Historic and Artistic Works recommends attaching a protective backing board available from a reputable framer to the reverse side of a painting to protect the work from exposure to environmental changes.
- Stable paintings, free of flaking or loose paint, can be carefully dusted with a soft bristle brush two or three times a year. Use extreme care when working with your paintings.
- Consult a conservator for repair or cleaning.

Storage Solutions

- Paintings and fine art are generally best preserved by proper display in your home, away from light, moisture, and heat.
- If you must store paintings, place a stiff art board, such as Foam-Cor board, on either side of the painting. An interior closet is a good place to store your painting. Place it where it will not be bumped or disturbed. Avoid attics, basements, and garages.

Cautions

- Avoid heat, soot, and smoke. The focal point over your mantle may not be the best place for valued artwork.
- Avoid damp. Do not display original art in bathrooms.
- Avoid direct sunlight or display lighting.
- Use great care when handling artwork, be careful not to bump, drop, or damage the work.

Tips

- Consider using UV protection glass when reframing works under glass.
- Museums recommend rotating displays of valuable pieces—six months on display, six months resting in storage—to prevent overexposure to environmental elements.

CHINA, GLASSWARE, AND COLLECTIBLES

I am an absolute fiend for china. I know that I don't need any more dishes, but I truly enjoy displaying and serving meals on different dishes as the whim and season strikes. My sister is the exact opposite. She has one set of all-purpose china and hesitates to add another. I've decided to be her family china shop, just in case she ever changes her mind.

Kitchenware, tableware, and decorative items made of ceramics, glass, crystal, porcelain, and earthenware all require similar care and storage. Vintage and antique pieces will need hand washing and drying; use care with hand-painted china and collectible figurines. Most antique china is not dishwasher, microwave, or oven safe.

Care

- Cushion your sink and countertop with thick towels when cleaning or handling your collection.
- Do not wrap china in newspaper or acidic newsprint paper for long-term storage; this can cause discoloration. Use acid-free, lignin-free tissue instead.

Storage Solutions

- Store china you use frequently in a buffet or china closet. Place a protective pad between plates as a cushion.
- Don't hang china cups by their handle on cup hooks. Dangling cups can be easily bumped and knocked into each other, which will cause chips.
- Store cups upright on their bottom rim. If you must stack cups, cushion cups with a thin pad or layer of acid-free, lignin-free tissue paper.
- If china is especially delicate or will be in long-term storage, keep it in padded, compartmentalized china cases available at housewares stores.

Cautions

- Use care with repaired items. Old glues are often weak and dry, causing pieces to break off again.
- Consult a professional to repair important pieces.

Tips

- Make your own plate and cup pads from coffee filter papers, paper towels, or felt. Avoid plastic.
- Create a photo album of your favorite pieces to enjoy, share, and itemize your collection for insurance purposes.

FURNITURE

When it comes to furniture (and lots of other stuff, actually) it's best to do no harm. Resist the temptation to remake a rocker into a standard-legged chair, trim a tabletop to fit a corner, or lower a cabinet by removing the claw feet. By respecting the integrity of the original piece, you also retain the best chance of preserving its value.

Care

- Wood furniture: Clean carefully; use only solid paste wax on clear-varnished wooden furniture, applied no more than once a year. Furniture polish and oils are not recommended because they tend to dry out the wood or create a gummy surface that attracts dirt and dust.
- Modern furniture: Use appropriate cleaning materials for mid-century furniture made of metal, Formica, or vinyl.
- Upholstered furniture: Clean fabric using the brush or upholstery attachment of your vacuum cleaner at the appropriate setting.

Storage Solutions

- Furniture is easily damaged. Often, the best place to store your heirloom pieces is within your living areas at the same environmental conditions that are comfortable for you.
- For fragile pieces, consider placing furniture in low-traffic areas, like a guest room or living room corner.
- If you must store furniture outside your house, avoid attics, basements, and garages whenever possible. Extremes in temperature and humidity, as well as exposure to insects and pests, can quickly damage your pieces.

Cautions

- Place furniture out of direct light and away from heating and air-conditioning registers.
- Spray furniture polish is easy to use and convenient, but it is a poor choice in caring for wood furniture. Use a clean, slightly damp dust cloth instead.
- Use great care when moving furniture. Cushion corners, legs, and awkward pieces before lifting. Remove loose pieces, such as finials, drawers, and drop leaves, and replace them after the furniture is in place.

MUSICAL INSTRUMENTS

"Use it or lose it" is archivist Don Williams's recommendation for musical instruments. Williams notes that regularly playing an instrument is the best way to monitor function and needed repair. Without proper maintenance, that violin or brass horn can easily lose its function to make music and become simply another interesting artifact. Care for individual items will depend on the nature of the instrument—stringed, wind, percussion. Take time to learn about your instrument and consult a conservationist for detailed instructions.

Care

- The Smithsonian Museum Conservation Institute offers links to many references for the specific care of various musical instruments **<www.si.edu/mci/english/learn_more/ taking_care/musinst.html>.**
- Maintain a stable environment; avoid fluctuations in temperature and humidity.
- Wash your hands before handling or playing.

Storage Solutions

- Hire professionals to move any large instruments, such as a piano or organ.
- Keep any securing straps in place.
- Maintain instrument storage cases; vacuum the interior and dust the exterior. Treat metal hardware to keep it free from rust.

Cautions

- Handle instruments carefully.
- Remove jewelry when handling to avoid scratching the instrument.

QUILTS AND SAMPLERS

Many family archives contain heirloom quilts and samplers. If you are lucky enough to have these treasures, take the time to preserve them for future generations.

Care

- Display quilts and other textiles on a rotating schedule; four to six months on display and the rest of the year "resting" in storage.
- Use a low-power, handheld vacuum for regular cleaning. Work slowly, avoid rubbing back and forth. Vacuum fragile fabrics through a fiberglass screen.
- Wash your hands and remove rings when working with textiles.
- Do not eat, smoke, or drink near your collection.
- Carefully support textiles when moving them from room to room.

Storage Solutions

- Select a cool, dry room with good air circulation for storing textiles. Avoid attics, basements, and garages.
- When possible, store textiles flat. Small pieces can be layered with archival tissue and placed inside an archival storage box.
- Large items, such as quilts, should be rolled to avoid creases. Use an archival tube to support the center; add cushioning with archival tissue to protect the surface. Use a piece of clean

washed muslin longer than the roll to form a protective outer layer. Roll the muslin around the item one and a half times, tucking in the ends at the end of the tube. Use cotton twill tape or muslin strips to tie the covering in place.

- Textiles may also be stored on display. The best mounts and hanging methods will depend on the type of textile. Generally, quilts and large stable items can be hung with Velcro strips or from a hand-sewn hanging sleeve. Supports and strainers can be used to distribute weight and help with displaying textiles. Consult the Textile Museum website, **<www.textilemuseum.org>**, for information about specific items.

Cautions

- Ideal climate for storing textiles is 65ºF–70ºF and 50–55 percent humidity.
- Light, heat, pollution, and high humidity will speed the deterioration of textiles.
- Wet cloth is weak; be careful to support quilts or clothing if they become wet.
- Do not try to clean textiles yourself. Consult a conservator.
- Examine textiles regularly for mold, mildew, and pests and treat immediately.

Tips

Under some conditions, it is appropriate to consider framing a textile behind glass or Plexiglas, which contains a UV filter to reduce damage from light. Framing may be a good option if:

- the item will be displayed in natural daylight
- dirt and dust are a problem
- the item will be displayed in an area where smoking is allowed

CLOTHING AND UNIFORMS

My father's parents weren't great savers. They were practical people who took good care of their things and didn't acquire more than they needed. When their home sold, we were surprised to uncover a small green trunk.

Inside the trunk, carefully wrapped in plastic dry cleaning bags, was my grandfather's uniform and gear from his years as a doughboy in World War I. My grandmother's meticulous housekeeping surely contributed to the excellent preservation of the trunk and its contents, although today's archival experts would not recommend using dry cleaning plastic as a storage material.

The key is always cleanliness and common sense. Grandmother cleaned the wool greatcoat and jacket before placing it in the trunk. The leather leggings were oiled and wrapped inside a similar pair of leggings made of stout canvas. Anything metal had been removed from the uniform for storage elsewhere.

Almost everyone has at least one sentimental clothing item, such as a wedding dress, christening gown, or letterman's jacket. Care for clothing according to the type of fabric, age of the garment, and overall fragility.

Care

- Wash your hands and remove rings when working with any textile.
- Remove metal pins, bars, or badges for storing elsewhere.
- Clean uniforms and clothing before storing. Dry cleaning may cause excessive drying to older fabrics; gently vacuum with a vinyl fabric screen over the nozzle on the low-volume upholstery setting.
- Examine clothing regularly for traces of pests, mold, and mildew and treat immediately.

Storage Solutions

- Select a cool, dry room with good air circulation for storing textiles. Avoid attics, basements, and garages.
- Clothing, such as wedding dresses, uniforms, and christening gowns, can be hung for storage if they are in good condition. The items should be freshly laundered. Wrap wooden hangers in polyester quilt batting covered with a muslin sleeve to give the garment more support. Stuff a pleated piece of archival tissue in garment sleeves and legs to support the fabric. Place the entire garment in a muslin garment bag of the same size as the garment. Do not use plastic or vinyl garment bags.

Cautions

- The ideal climate for storing textiles is 65ºF–70ºF and 50–55 percent humidity.
- Light, heat, pollution, and high humidity will speed the deterioration of textiles.

MILITARY INSIGNIA, SCOUTING MEMORABILIA, AND FLAGS

Some of my best childhood memories recall adventures with friends in Girl Scouts and the challenges of new experiences. With no daughter to follow my Girl Scout footsteps, I was delighted when both sons joined Boy Scouts and eventually achieved the Eagle Scout rank. As they outgrew their scout uniforms, I snipped off the badges and arranged them in a shadow box to mark their achievement. Now, they're the perfect decoration for my grandson's bedrooms, and hopefully an inspiration to the next generation of scouts!

If you choose to remove insignia and pins from military or scouting uniforms, know how to care for the different items. Many options are available today for preserving uniforms, flags, and medals depending on your intended use or display. Whatever you select, do your best with the time and resources you have available.

My grandmother wisely removed metal pins and bars from my grandfather's doughboy uniform, but his rank and unit patches remained securely attached. You will want to do the same with any type of military or scouting uniform.

Care

- Treat medals like coins or jewelry; keep free of dust by gently cleaning with a dry cloth or a soft bristle brush.
- Care for fabric patches and badges like clothing. Use a vacuum to remove dust.
- Handle with care. Wear cotton gloves to protect items from the natural oils of your skin.

Storage Solutions

- Medals, badges, patches, and pins can be stored in glass shadow boxes, or beneath glass coffee table tops.
- If archival storage is preferred, use archival collection boxes with acid-free, lignin-free tissue for cushioning individual items.
- Store items in a temperate location inside your home. Avoid attics, basements, and garages.
- Flags and pennants should be rolled in archival tissue paper and placed in a clean muslin sleeve.

Cautions

- Patches and ribbons fade easily; keep away from sunlight and UV light.
- Traces of dirt, grass, or stains will hasten the deterioration of fabric.
- Avoid nonarchival plastic sleeves for storing medals, patches, and pins.
- Don't use a wool backing to display medals. Wool contains sulfur that will eventually damage the medal. Cotton is a better option.
- Museums recommend rotating displays—six months on display, six months resting in storage—to prevent overexposure to environmental elements.
- Riker Mounts are popular display options but are intended for short-term use only. Use similar archival-grade display cases for long-term display or storage. See the Resources section at the end of the chapter.

Tip

- Enjoy and share your collection by combining storage and display in glass front cases.

WATCHES AND JEWELRY

Whether you inherit one piece of jewelry or an entire chest full, one pocket watch or several, do try to keep sets intact.

Storage Solutions

- Invest in a jewelry box with multiple compartments and a lid to protect your collection from dust and breakage.
- To minimize wear and damage, rotate favorite pieces of jewelry or watches between storage and your jewelry box. Always clean pieces before storing.
- Consider storing collections in archival compartment boxes with acid-free tissue for cushioning.

Cautions

- Consult a jeweler for cleaning and repair advice for specific pieces of jewelry.
- Use a soft cloth to keep jewelry clean.
- Keep timepieces in good working order.

Tips

- Collections are more valuable than individual items; whenever possible, try to keep a matching set intact. Keep cuff links with matching tie bars; keep matching earrings, bracelets, brooches, necklaces, and rings together.
- Use your digital camera or movie camera to make a visual record of your collection.
- Talk to your insurance agent about extra coverage to insure your valuable pieces against theft or loss.

TOYS, DOLLS, AND GAMES

It's hard to say good-bye to a favorite toy at any age; no wonder parents carefully pack away a scruffy stuffed dog or rag doll. Unwrapping Spot or Barbie decades later can bring back a flood of memories. The dolls from my childhood are definitely vintage, but just as definitely not highly collectable. I'm saving them to show a granddaughter one day, but I'm not investing in individual storage boxes for each doll. Instead, they all live together nestled in archival tissue like one big happy family inside one big archival box.

Care

- Wear white cotton gloves when handling stuffed animals and dolls to prevent the transfer of natural oils from your hands to the toys.
- Clean toys and dolls gently by vacuuming indirectly with a brush attachment and screen or coarse fabric diffuser (attach a square of vinyl window screen or piece of coarse fabric over the nozzle of the vacuum).
- Consult a conservator for advice about cleaning antique toys and dolls.

- Clean modern plastic and rubber dolls only with distilled water unless you know how a particular cleaner will react with the specific plastic or rubber material.

Storage Solutions

- Display stuffed animals and antique dolls in a dust-free place, such as a glass-front cabinet under low light. Keep the temperature under 70°F.
- Store clean stuffed animals and dolls wrapped in archival tissue or clean muslin and placed inside archival boxes with lids.
- Store vintage and modern dolls and plastic action figures in the dark, in a cool, dry, clean place with good air circulation.
- Board games and puzzles are usually made from high-wood pulp cardboard and paper. Keep separate from other papers and documents in temperate storage.
- Chess sets, Dominoes, Mah-jongg Tiles: Care for these sets according to the type of material they are made from. Keep clean and dust free if placed on display; store in archival containers.

Cautions

- Never clean a doll or toy unless you know the material it is made of and how it will react to your cleaning agent. When it doubt, use distilled water on a cotton swab. Always test any cleaner in an inconspicuous place.

Tip

- Display collectible action figures in a miniature curio cabinet. Make your own case from an archival glass-front shadow box.

METAL TOOLS AND OUTDOORS STUFF

My husband's eyes grew glazed as he peered inside the dark corners of Auntie's single car garage. The door may have been regularly lifted to the outside, but it was obvious that the junk lining the sides and against the far back hadn't been touched since it was quickly dumped there decades ago.

It looked like a Dumpster could make fast work of the accumulated debris, but what do I know? My husband latched on to a giant Rain Bird sprinkler, looked at me, and grinned. He knew my weakness. I do love that summertime sound—the *chuck, chuck, chuck, chuck, whirrrrrrr* of the Rain Bird sprinkler performing in various backyard symphonies. And, you just don't find 'em like that anymore.

If any gardeners or tool lovers in your family are involved in cleaning out a family home, I bet you brought home a few tools or outdoor garden items, too. Most of these are made of wood or metal, in varying stages of care, but with a bit of cleaning and polishing, you can safely move vintage items to your home for display in a collection, or just put them to use in your own backyard.

Care

- If your goal is to display interesting artifacts rather than preserve them, don't worry about removing all traces of rust and use. Do, however, remove dirt, insects, and old grass to extend the life of your treasure.
- If the tools are not valuable or in extremely poor repair, consider adapting Agway's garden tool care procedure: "Disassemble tools with metal parts first. Thoroughly clean metal surfaces with a wire brush, fine steel wool or medium grit sandpaper; lubricate annually with a light synthetic oil. Clean and smooth wooden handles with light sandpaper and treat with boiled linseed oil."
- Keep tools dry.
- Wipe tools and metal objects with a clean, damp cloth. Dry thoroughly before storing indoors.

Storage Solutions

- Store metal and cast iron tools in a super-dry place. Heat will not damage most metal, but humidity will encourage rust.
- Store and display small items, such as doorknobs, keys, or hardware, in archival artifact boxes.

Cautions

- Do not display or store valuable tools outdoors.
- For tools with metal parts and wooden handles, clean each part appropriately and choose a compromise in storage.

RESOURCES

Specialty Artifact Storage

GAYLORD <www.gaylord.com> (800) 448-6160
Archival storage for artifacts, collectibles, documents, film, photographs, textiles, and natural history collections.

HOLLINGER METAL EDGE <www.hollingermetaledge.com> (800) 862-2228
Wide variety of archival storage materials; good source for hard-to-find paper file folder inserts.

RIKER MOUNTS < www.rikermounts.net>
Non-archival display option for short-term display only. Use similar archival grade options available from archival suppliers for long-term storage.

Preserving Family Collections

American Institute for Conservation of Historic and Artistic Works
<www.conservation-us.org >

Sally Jacobs, The Practical Archivist **<www.practicalarchivist.com>**

Military Memorabilia

American War Library, How to Display U.S. Military Ribbons and Medals
<www.americanwarlibrary.com/display>

State Historical Society of Iowa, Preserving Flags, Uniforms, and Medals
<www.iowahistory.org/archives/technical-assistance/preserving-flags-uniforms-and-medals.html>

Quilts and Textiles

International Quilt Study Center & Museum
<www.quiltstudy.org/about_us/questions_answers/care.html>

The Textile Museum, Guidelines for the Care of Textiles
<www.textilemuseum.org/care/brochures/guidelines.htm>

University of Nebraska, Care and Conservation of Heirloom Textiles
<www.ianrpubs.unl.edu/epublic/live/g1682/build/g1682.pdf>

PART 2

Break the Paper Habit

Like many researchers, I have a love/hate relationship with paper. As a family historian, I cherish the touch and smell of old paper and the knowledge that a document can be picked up and read by anyone, almost anytime. The scrawl of fading ink over the uneven texture of rag paper makes me smile. The firm stroke of pencil on school newsprint conjures a vision of childhood determination.

Then I turn to look around my home office and sigh in frustration. At times, I feel like I am being buried under a paper mountain. Magazines, journals, charts, pedigree printouts, census copies, conference notes, and lists. Do we really need to keep all this paper?

If you're like me, you may not be ready to completely abandon paper, but you may be ready use your computer to handle some of the heavy lifting when it comes to document file management.

In this section, we'll look at ways to make your computer a more efficient research assistant and discover how to stretch your technology skills and budget to maximize your research hours.

CHAPTER 9 ORGANIZE AND DIGITIZE YOUR PAPER DOCUMENTS: It's not practical to eliminate all paper files, but going digital saves storage space and search time. This chapter shows you how to move toward a paperless genealogy office step by step, from scanning to storage.

CHAPTER 10 DIGITIZE YOUR FAMILY ARCHIVE: Digital copies preserve heirloom originals and give you a working copy for research and creative projects. This chapter presents sample workflows to help you safely create digital copies of archive materials.

CHAPTER 11 ORGANIZE YOUR PAPER FILES: Do you feel buried in a mountain of genealogy papers? This chapter offers practical ideas for a personalized filing system to suit your research style and experience.

CHAPTER 12 ORGANIZE YOUR COMPUTER: Your computer can be a top-notch filing clerk and research assistant with strategies in this chapter for a consistent file-naming system, simple folder structure, and scheduled backup plan.

9

Organize and Digitize
Your Paper Documents

The notion of a paperless genealogy life might sound like a good idea, but for most researchers, eliminating all paper isn't a practical option. Anyone who has read or handled a centuries-old document has a certain degree of confidence in the longevity of paper records that has yet to be matched by digital files. Yet there are many great benefits to using digital documents:

- Digital files take up less physical storage space.
- Images can be enlarged or enhanced for greater readability.
- Copies can easily be sent via e-mail.
- Files can be archived in more than one location.
- Files can be printed on archival paper to create a paper archive copy.
- Images can be linked to more than one project or person.
- Files can be quickly located and retrieved by the computer.
- An automated back-up program for computer files will create an archived digital version.

As the caretaker of my family's heirloom documents, I would never recommend digitizing old records and destroying the originals. In fact, I'm an advocate for creating your own paper heirloom originals of some unique records.

Think about your genealogy files as two different record types—**archive original documents** that you want to physically preserve and store, and **working documents** used every day that are more temporary in nature. A different digital routine is needed for each record type.

This chapter offers ideas for using digital files with your genealogy research and converting from paper to digital. Resources will help you find scanning and software solutions as you move toward digital filing.

ARCHIVE ORIGINAL DOCUMENTS

Heirloom original documents are the treasures of your archive; they don't really belong mixed in with your office files at all. Instead, they should be organized in appropriate archival storage containers in your family archive.

The wonderful 1891 baptism record of my grandmother Arline is a document worth preserving, along with her colorful marriage certificates and many letters. I consider these original ancestor records as Archive Documents. My overall goal is to preserve the originals; I feel this is best accomplished by creating a digital copy of the documents by scanning or photographing them and then preserving the originals in archival storage.

I can reference the digital versions as often as I want without disturbing the originals. The digital copies also provide working copies that can be manipulated for easier viewing, transcribing, and sharing. And finally, digital copies can also become digital archive images, which preserve the information in case disaster destroys the hard copy original.

WORKING DOCUMENTS

All the other paper in my office, including magazines, journals, and printed material, is temporary. Most family historians have considerably more paper working documents than archive original documents. It's the temporary paper that covers the desk, the shelves, and maybe even the floor. Digital versions of these documents can save space, time, money, and sanity.

My home office may still be home to piles of paper, but much of it is on its way to being recycled. I don't generate hard copies of reports or database information because the reports are outdated as soon as I enter more information. Instead, I only print copies as needed, or when a project is completed and I want to create my own Archive Document of a digital file.

Now that we've established that we're not getting rid of archive original documents, does the prospect of letting go of all your working papers still scare you? If so, maybe one of these myths about going digital is holding you back:

You Can't Break the Paper Habit

Paper is how you've always saved information. It's true: Documents need to be maintained for future reference, but they don't necessarily need to remain as ink on paper. Don't miss out on a time- and space-saving opportunity simply because you don't think you can change. You don't have to go digital overnight. There's nothing wrong with moving slowly when it comes to handling important information. Start slowly by trying to keep one or two working documents digital only. Then add more to the mix. You may eventually scan and digitize all your files, but if you don't, that's okay to. Start from today and move forward one small step at a time.

Digitization is Expensive

Computers, scanners, and hard drive space aren't free, but neither is physical file storage. Remember the last time you purchased a file cabinet and supplies? The technology required for digitization and digital storage becomes more affordable each year. A one terabyte (TB) external hard drive now costs less than a good quality file cabinet and, although it fits in the palm of your hand, it can store the same amount of information! You don't need a lot of fancy technology to move toward digital storage; all you need is a computer and some kind of external backup storage.

Have you ever paid a moving company to move your files to a new home or storage facility? It can be hard to downsize your lifestyle when physical files consume a good percentage of your living space. Accommodating those physical files may be a hidden expense that is far greater than the cost of technology for digitizing.

You Don't Know How to "Go Digital"

This may be true now, but by the time you finish reading this chapter, you'll have the information you need to go digital with your working files.

BREAKING THE PAPER HABIT IN SEVEN STEPS

If you've put off going digital because paper is how you've always stored your information, try these seven steps to break free from your paper habit.

1. PICK A START DATE. Businesses recognize the value of knowing exactly when they shifted from paper to digital; it's easier to find things. It also makes the task of moving away from paper much more realistic. On the other hand, many genealogists have been researching for decades, and hope to be enjoying their work for decades to come. You don't have to convert thirty years of paper documents to digital files before you can begin to use electronic file management. Begin by saving new information as digital documents and filing according to your file scheme. Your start date is the date you will go digital moving forward. Your old files can remain paper until you are ready to digitize them (and if that day never comes, that's okay).

Set the date ahead of time and give yourself a chance to get used to the idea and to practice your digital file routine. Select a meaningful date, if possible, such as your birthdate, New Year's Day, Tax Day—anything that will be easy to remember.

2. PRINT LESS. Whenever you need to keep information, choose to save a digital version instead of printing a paper copy. Mac users have a built-in feature through the Print command to save files as PDFs. Select Save as PDF and give the file a meaningful file name according to your chosen file-naming scheme. PC users may need additional software for this task; see the Resources section at the end of this chapter.

Organize your saved PDF files as you would any other document and file in the appropriate folder and subfolder.

3. USE A CONSISTENT FILE-NAMING SCHEME. If you've been using a computer for any length of time, you probably already have a file-naming scheme in place. If not, or if you feel like you need a better system, investigate different options and find one that works for you before beginning a full-scale digital file management program.

Some genealogists find that a combination of Surname, Date, and File ID works well for digital files; others use a numerical reference number that corresponds to paper files. Find more information on file-naming schemes in chapter twelve.

4. KISS, KEEP IT SUPER SIMPLE. Keep your system easy and intuitive. Don't be tempted by fancy, hard-to-remember schemes. Develop a workflow that suits your own personal style, and tweak it until it's nearly effortless.

5. POST A WORKFLOW CHEAT SHEET. Post a simple list to remind you of your paper workflow and file-naming scheme. This can be a real timesaver for those of us who research in bits and spurts on weekends and vacations.

6. CELEBRATE YOUR DIGITAL BIRTHDAY. Every year on the anniversary of your digital switch, evaluate your current system and upgrade if necessary. This is especially important if you use CDs for external storage; CDs deteriorate over time and older formats should be upgraded to remain compatible with new operating systems.

7. PURGE THE PAPER. No doubt, you have a considerable amount of paper sitting on your desk right now. As you get more comfortable with going digital, how do you handle the paper pile? You have two choices: digitize or purge. Do you really need to keep the paper copy? Is the information readily available online or in a public resource?

If you must keep the material because it's a current working document or valuable reference material, ask yourself if it needs to be kept in paper form. If not, scan the paper and throw away the original. Apply your file-naming scheme to the new digital document and be confident that you can retrieve the information as needed.

Scanning paper documents is a big job. A flat-bed scanner is great for digitizing fragile documents and photographs, but it's slow and cumbersome for hundreds of pages of standard-sized office paper. Consider using a sheet-fed scanner or hiring a student to digitize a large project.

SCANNER OPTIONS

As you go paperless, you'll need tools to help convert your paper files. A home office scanner is a workhorse in the paperless office. For mobile scanning, you may already own two of the most useful digitization tools: a mobile phone with a camera and a digital camera.

Not all scanners are the same, or can manage all tasks equally well. Most genealogists rely on a flat-bed, photo-quality scanner as an all-purpose office tool suitable for digitizing both heirloom documents and office files. A flat-bed scanner may be the best option for digitizing fragile material, but it's an inefficient choice for setting up a paperless office. If possible, add a fast, sheet-fed scanner to your office equipment and watch your paper mountain disappear. Special Optical Character Recognition (OCR) software can convert scanned documents into searchable text making it even easier to find the information you need. For portable scanning, rely on your digital camera for fast, efficient copies.

Here are several choices to help you digitize your documents:

Office All-in-One Scanner

Paper isn't the only thing that can pile up in a home office. Consider consolidating office equipment too with an all-in-one printer-fax-copier-scanning machine. These devices typically offer a flat-bed scanning surface (if so, scanning is the same on this device as on a flat-bed scanner), and may include a sheet-fed attachment as well.

Look for software with variable file formats and scanning resolutions. Third-party software can add additional features, if desired.

Flat-Bed Photo Scanner

Use a flat-bed scanner to digitize fragile documents and photographs from your family archive to make digital master copies. When purchasing a new scanner, look for one that is designed to scan both documents and photos, and comes with its own software. Software that offers batch-scanning features can make your project go faster.

Also consider the overall size of the flat-bed surface; you will want a scanner that accommodates a minimum 8½" × 11" sheet of paper. Many family history documents are legal-sized, so a scanning screen of at least 14" is even better.

If you plan to digitize negatives and slides, you will need a negative or slide carrier attachment to hold the transparencies above the glass bed of the scanner.

This equipment is not intended as a portable machine, although some researchers do tote their scanners to libraries and archives. Refer to your scanner manual to learn how to lock the scanning carriage before moving the machine.

Portable Flat-Bed Scanner

These machines are about the size of a netbook computer and weigh less than a pound. Power comes from standard AA batteries; files are saved to a SD Media Card.

These pint-size workhorses offer many of the features of a full-sized, flat-bed scanner, but be prepared for a few trade-offs. Models I tested offer JPG scanning only and a glass scanning surface of 5" × 7". You can work around these limitations by converting JPG images to TIFF to create Digital Master Copies and use the unique see-through feature to scan oversized items. Built-in software stitches multiple scans together to form one complete image from several individual files.

While the small screen size can be inconvenient, it easily accommodates the popular 4" × 6" snapshots in many home collections. Portability and ease of use make these little scanners a great option if you travel often or need to go to a family member's house to digitize photos. Remember to take extra batteries and memory cards with you.

Portable Wand Scanner

If you are looking for the smallest scanning solution, a wand scanner may suit your needs, although most devices require a steady hand and some practice for optimal results. You will also be limited in file format, resolution, and scan image size.

The wand is typically a square tool about the width of a sheet of letter-sized paper. The wand is passed over the page to create the scanned image. This option is best for library researchers who need to copy bound materials for off-site study.

Portable Sheet-Fed Scanner

Mobile researchers may also be interested in a small sheet-fed scanner that offers portability, speed, and ease of use. This kind of scanner feeds paper through the machine over the scanning head and is best for office and research documents, not for heirloom originals.

Sheet-fed scanners, like home printers, are susceptible to paper jams that may bend, tear, or damage documents. You might not care if your lecture notes are accidentally torn, but it could be a disaster if the only photo of your grandfather was scratched or bent beyond recognition.

Some sheet-fed scanners are small enough to be portable, yet sturdy enough for moderate home office use. When bundled with OCR software, this scanner can be an efficient tool in converting your office from paper to digital documents.

Mobile Phone or Tablet Camera

A mobile smartphone equipped with camera and e-mail capabilities can manage a great deal of information. This portable pocket "scanner" is especially useful for digitizing notes, receipts, and other business or personal information. In a pinch, use your smart phone camera to snap gravestone photos or take the place of a library copier.

Some mobile phones and most tablet devices can expand their capabilities with inexpensive specialized applications, called apps. From scanning to photo-enhancement, these programs can help you maximize the usefulness of your mobile devices for genealogy.

After taking a digital image of the item with your smart phone camera, you will need to move the image to your computer for file naming and file storage. Learn the most efficient way to move pictures from your phone to your computer. Some options include transfer via wireless home network, sending a file to yourself as an e-mail attachment, saving to an online service such as

Dropbox or iCloud, or transfer via USB cable. Most smartphone cameras record JPG file format, so you may also want to convert any special images to TIFF format for preservation.

Digital Camera

A digital camera is the family historian's go-to tool. It can snap photos at the family reunion and capture a full image of Aunt May's scrapbook.

Add a tripod or copy stand to your equipment and you have a portable scanner. Travel with extra batteries and memory cards to minimize downtime. Get around the limitations of the JPG file format by always converting and saving a TIFF Digital Master Copy when you get back to your computer.

When purchasing a digital camera for genealogy work, a few features will come in especially handy:

- a self-timer so that you can be included in group photos
- buttons and knobs sized for your hands and fingers
- a screw mount for tripod or copy stand
- easy-to-use menu to turn off Auto Flash (You will get better results copying documents in natural light.)

I like a compact camera that fits easily in my research bag without adding too much weight or bulk so I am not tempted to leave it behind.

Computer Webcam

You might not think of your computer camera for digitizing, but it does a fairly good job for quick scans of office documents, especially small receipts, business cards, and notes. These files can be added to your working digital documents files to replace the bits and pieces of notepaper that create clutter.

PC users with a webcam can use the accompanying webcam software to capture and save digital images. Mac users have the built-in iSight camera for taking photos; if images are mirror reversed, use the Flip Photo option under the Edit menu to correctly view the image.

Not all digital projects require the same quality images or merit the time and effort required for full 600 dpi TIFF format files. Choose the digitizing method that best suits your purpose as you work toward minimizing paper clutter and becoming a more effective family historian.

HOW TO SCAN WITH A FLAT-BED SCANNER

1. CLEAN YOUR SCANNER GLASS. Begin each scanning session by cleaning the glass bed of your scanner with a soft microfiber cloth. Lightly dampen the cloth with water or glass-cleaning solution.

2. CLEAN YOUR PHOTOS. If you are scanning photos, use a soft artist's brush to lightly brush off any loose dirt. For more thorough cleaning, use special photo cleaners available at a photo specialty store. Many problems can be corrected with photo-editing software, leaving your original images untouched.

Never use an office eraser to get rid of marks or smudges.

3. SET THE FORMAT TYPE: FILM (SLIDE OR NEGATIVE), PHOTOGRAPH, OR TEXT DOCUMENT. On many scanners, as you begin to make selections, the software takes over other decisions for you.

4. SET THE FILE FORMAT: JPG VS. TIFF. Most point-and-click digital cameras record photos in JPG format, a compact, efficient file format that is widely accepted for photo sharing, editing, and e-mailing. Unfortunately, JPG is also a lossy format, meaning that each time the file is saved, some information is lost as the file is compressed to minimize the total file size. Most of us can't detect the loss after one or two rounds of saving, but at one point, the image will become filled with artifacts from the compression and noticeable degradation will become very obvious.

Museums and archives recommend using TIFF format when archiving historic documents because it is a lossless format that is very good at saving original information even when the file is saved many times. These institutions have determined that the trade-off in large file size is worth the added value of preserving the original image through multiple versions.

For family historians, TIFF is a good format for your Archive Original Documents and Photographs; however, to use this file in a genealogy database or post it to a Web page, the TIFF file must be converted to the JPG format. This is a simple one-step process that can be added to your scanning workflow (see more information in chapter ten for TIFF and JPG archive workflows).

Working documents or transitory files should be digitized and saved as PDF (Portable Document Format) or JPG files.

5. SET THE RESOLUTION, OR DOTS PER INCH (DPI). You have probably heard a lot of talk about dpi for scanning: Some people insist on scanning family photos at "the highest possible resolution." Others suggest 300 dpi, and still others say it doesn't really matter. What should you do?

Dots per inch (dpi) is relevant to scanning because it sets the ratio at which the original image is converted from printed dots to digital pixels. You could scan all your originals in the highest dpi available, but this would result in extremely large files and likely little improvement in quality. A better solution is to choose a dpi that will result in good quality and reasonable file size.

A 600 dpi scan of a 4" × 6" print will have enough information to print a good quality 8" × 10" enlargement, but when my original is extremely small, I like to increase the scanning dpi even higher. The typical group photo or a photo booth print starts out with small-scale faces. When I know that I will want to print an image considerably larger than the original, or when I plan detailed retouching, I set my scanner for 1200 dpi scanning. If you are digitizing negatives or slides, scan these images between 2400 dpi and 3200 dpi to ensure that you are capturing the full range of data in a slide or negative. Find specific ideas for negative scanning in the Resources

SCANNING GUIDELINES

	Recommended Scanner Type	DPI	Format	Color	
Letters, Documents	Flat-bed or Digital Camera	300	TIFF or JPG	24-bit color	
Photographs	Flat-bed	600	TIFF	24-bit color	
Album Pages	Flat-bed or Digital Camera	600	TIFF	24-bit color	
Small Books	Flat-bed or Digital Camera	600	TIFF	24-bit color	
Tintypes, Daguerreotypes	Flat-bed	1200	TIFF	24-bit color	
Negatives, Slides	Flat-bed Scanner with Carrier or Special Scanner	2400 to 3200	TIFF	Transparency	
Quilts and Other Textiles	Digital Camera		JPG		Convert and Save TIFF Archive Copy
3-D Artifacts	Digital Camera		JPG		Convert and Save TIFF Archive Copy
Maps, Large Documents	Digital Camera		JPG		Convert and Save TIFF Archive Copy
Working Documents, Research, Receipts, etc.	Digital Camera, Mobile Phone Camera, or Scanner	300 for printing, 72 for display	JPG	24-bit color	

Note: Convert and save images made by a digital camera in JPG format to TIFF format copies for your Digital Master Archive.

section at the end of this chapter. See the Scanning Guidelines chart for recommended dpi for scans of various photos and document types.

6. SET THE COLOR CHOICE. Your scanner may allow different color choices, such as CMYK, sRGB, Adobe RGB, Grayscale, Black and White, or others, along with options for 8 or 16 bits/channel.

I set my scanner at the standard sRGB (Red, Green, and Blue) at 8 bits/channel (24 bits total) and am satisfied with the results for my archive images.

Scan all items in full color, including newsprint and black-and-white photographs. Your file size will be larger, but the color channels will capture shading and detail with greater clarity.

7. TURN ON DUST AND SCRATCH REMOVAL, IF DESIRED. This may be called Digital ICE on some scanners.

8. SET YOUR FILE-NAMING AND FILE-SAVING PREFERENCES. Save images to a separate folder and then input to photo software for tagging and converting TIFF to JPG.

9. PREVIEW THE IMAGE. Check for orientation and framing. Adjust if necessary.

10. SCAN.

DIGITIZING ARCHIVE ORIGINAL DOCUMENTS

Family archive documents are digitized with three goals in mind:

1. TO PROTECT THE ORIGINAL. A quality digital duplicate can reduce the need to view the original document.

2. TO REPLACE THE ORIGINAL. A digital copy can provide a duplicate image copy to serve in place of the original in case of loss, irreparable damage, or deterioration, and to produce further paper copies.

3. TO PROVIDE ACCESS TO THE INFORMATION CONTAINED IN THE ORIGINAL. A digital copy can be viewed, edited, shared, and used in many ways without handling the original.

Each of these goals require the highest quality duplicate image, so it's important to use a scanner that can provide the best possible digital image.

Family archive documents destined to become digital master copies are best digitized using either a flat-bed scanner or a digital camera. The resulting digital files should be saved in the TIFF format; see the Scanning Guidelines chart for appropriate settings.

DIGITIZING WORKING DOCUMENTS

Genealogy working documents are digitized mostly for efficiency. Originals often exist in other repositories in multiple versions. The purpose in digitizing journal articles, notes, and receipts is primarily:

1. TO PROVIDE ACCESS TO INFORMATION. Digital copies can be transmitted electronically and accessed off-site.

2. TO PROVIDE EFFICIENT AND ECONOMICAL STORAGE AND RETRIEVAL. Digital versions take a fraction of the storage space required for physical files and can be quickly retrieved with computer search software. In addition, obsolete files are easily deleted or archived.

These files are not destined to become heirloom digital documents; they are valued primarily for the information they contain. It's most efficient to use a digitization process for these documents that is easy, efficient, and economical.

Most genealogy office documents require only that the information be readable and perhaps, searchable. A traditional flat-bed scanner isn't necessary for these documents. Instead, a fast, sheet-fed office scanner or a cell-phone camera will provide suitable results. Use 300 dpi for documents you may want to print; 72 dpi for items you only need to view on a computer monitor. Use standard settings on your digital camera. It's not necessary to use the archival TIFF format for everyday files; use the more compact JPG format.

You'll save a lot of time, stress, and money if you let go of the notion that everything needs to be digitized to the same standards. The nineteenth-century photograph of your great-grandmother is a family archive document that deserves the time and patience required for a high-quality image from your flat-bed scanner. Your handwritten research notes for last month's genealogy workshop will be easily read from a photo snapped with your cell phone camera and enlarged on your computer monitor, or scanned with a speedy sheet-fed scanner.

RESOURCES

Scanner Manufacturers

Canon **<www.canon.com>**
Epson **<www.epson.com>**
Flip-Pal Mobile Scanner **<www.flip-pal.com>**
Fujitsu ScanSnap **<www.fujitsu.com>**
Hewlett-Packard **<www.hp.com>**
Visioneer **<www.visioneer.com>**

Scanner Reviews

CNET **<www.cnet.com>**
PC Magazine **<www.pcmag.com>**
Imaging Resource **<www.imaging-resource.com>**

Scanning Information

Library of Congress **<www.digitalpreservation.gov/personalarchiving/>**

Digital Images and Genealogy by Ken Watson
<www.rideau-info.com/photos/genealogy-home.html>

Paperless Office Software

Devon Technologies DevonThink (Mac) **<www.devontechnologies.com>**

Ironic Yep (Mac) **<www.yepthat.com>**

Mariner Software Paperless (Mac, PC) **<www.marinersoftware.com>**

Nuance PaperPort (PC) **<www.paperport.com>**

PC Print to PDF Software

CutePDF **<www.cutepdf.com>**

Microsoft Word Save as PDF free add-on **<www.microsoft.com>**

PDFCreator **<sourceforge.net>**

10

Digitize Your Family Archive

My mom and I enjoyed a rather peculiar ritual when she came to visit. We cleared off the dining table, washed our hands, and brought out a box or two of old letters. Unlike Mom's sister, who was squeamish about reading other people's mail, Mom and I had no such qualms. Who needed a movie when we had the stories and half-tales scrawled in my grandmother's familiar hand?

We laughed over the jilted girlfriend who wrote "leave it to a dirty unprincipled jealous woman to do you dirt!" and cried when we found the post mortem photograph of the little girl who was Mom's great-aunt.

Letters, documents, photos, receipts, and albums were all packed away in my grandmother Arline's trunk when she died in 1967, but Arline took steps to preserve the stories they held.

First, she managed to preserve not only the letters she had received from family and friends throughout much of her life, she also saved the letters written to her husband and to her mother.

Second, and most importantly, she wrote lavish and extensive notes on the reverse side of photographs. We wouldn't use ink today for those notes, but frankly, I don't mind at all that she did! I am just grateful for the information.

Last, by saving news clippings and related correspondence, she tried to place people and events in the larger context of her times.

This meant, of course, that the material in Arline's archive was handled by many people—herself, her mother, other family members, my mom, me. All that touching, folding, and unfolding can be hard on an old letter. I wasn't about to restrict Mom's access to her own mother's things, but I was able to minimize future damage by digitizing the material.

In this chapter, I share my experience scanning and indexing the letters, documents, and photos found in Arline's archive, and offer ideas for your own digitization project. Resources highlight helpful computer software for working with documents and images.

ORGANIZE YOUR FAMILY ARCHIVE CATALOG

So far, we've talked a lot about organizing the paper and computer files that clutter our home offices. But, what's the best system to organize the information we need to keep and easily retrieve?

As you sort and organize the materials in your family archive, you probably realize that you need some way to catalog the items you move into archival storage containers. An inventory list is helpful, but not the best solution when the collection numbers hundreds of items.

In two decades of working with my own family archive, I've developed a simple system to organize my collection and keep items accessible for various projects. Remember chapter one, when you wrote down your own goals and objectives for your family archive? Take out that list again and review it. Has anything changed? Do you want to add or delete anything? You will want to work toward your goals as you set up a digital archive of your physical family archive.

The most useful digital archive contains at least two forms of digital copies: a master copy and a working copy. A digital master copy is the digital equal of your heirloom original document or photograph. It can provide a replacement print if necessary, and can be used to create digital working copies for use in photobooks, transcriptions, and research. You will need both kinds of digital copies.

Are you a Creator? You will need access to the information as well as images of the items in your archive. For virtually all uses, a digital image can be used in place of the original archive document. You need digital master copies that are easy to find and use.

Are you a Curator? You are primarily interested in sorting, organizing, and preserving material; but a good curator needs access for research and study. You need a way to link original documents with digital copies to ensure the preservation of heirloom material.

Are you a Caretaker? You consider your job as a temporary one. You may be more interested in preservation than digitization, but be aware that after the material leaves your care, the information it contains is lost. You will have to rely on the next caretaker to pull out any information needed by future family members. Reconsider your role, and look into a digitizing service that can make digital master copies for you and your heirs.

To be most useful, digital master copies need to be easily linked to original material and easily accessed. Each item will need a unique identification. Identification could be either a meaningful name or a combination of letters and numbers. I recommend two different cataloging methods, depending on the size and scope of your collection. Small collections can be cataloged using a table in your word processor, or with a simple spreadsheet. Larger collections will benefit from the searching features of a custom database form or flexible spreadsheet.

You will need photo software that allows file conversion between JPG and TIFF file formats, and the ability to add metadata keywords and tags. Fortunately, computers are tailor-made for the job.

SAMPLE WORKFLOW FOR SMALL TO MEDIUM FAMILY ARCHIVE CATALOGS

For collections with fewer than a hundred or so items, it's possible to manage a catalog using either meaningful identification names or unique identification codes. If you anticipate your collection growing dramatically, consider using unique ID codes, explained in the Sample Workflow for Large Family Archive Catalogs.

I classify a small archive as one with up to one hundred documents, photos, or letters. A medium-sized archive has a few hundred items. The archive materials are held in a few archival storage boxes and folders by one person in one location.

The digital archive of can be stored on a computer hard drive or on an external disk. Back up all TIFF digital master copies to a second device. Make digital JPG copies to use for research and projects.

STEP 1. Organize the original archive folders and boxes by surname or year, whatever best fits your overall goals.

STEP 2. Create a new folder on your hard drive: *Family Archive Files.*

STEP 3. Inside this folder, create two sub-folders: Archive Digital Masters TIFF and Archive Digital JPG.

STEP 4. Scan each archive original document as a TIFF file and save to the folder named Archive Digital Masters TIFF. Use file names that correspond to your file folder system.

For folders and boxes organized by surname, you could try something like this: smith-john_1925_birthcert.tif.

For folders and boxes organized by date you could try something like this: 1925-06_smith-john_birthcert.tif.

Note: You may need to scan the front and back of many items; append the small letter *f* (front) or *r* (reverse) to your unique name or code.

STEP 5. Add the unique ID name to each item, either on the archival enclosure (paper or polyester archival folder) or written in pencil on the reverse side of the original document.

STEP 6. File the original document alphabetically by surname or chronologically by date. This is how the computer will sort your catalog listing, and having both systems match will make it quicker and easier to find items.

STEP 7. Open the TIFF file, apply metadata keywords and tags if desired. Save the file as a JPG format file and place this new file in the folder named Archive Digital JPG.

Use the same file name as the TIFF file and let the extension (.tif or .jpg) distinguish the different files.

STEP 8. Create a new catalog of the digitized items using a word processing table or spreadsheet, and save this catalog inside your main Family Archive folder on your computer.

Include columns and information for:

Item Description—brief description

Digital File Name—your new digital file name

Location of Original—where to find original document or photo

Keywords—names of people, places, events to aid in searches

Thumbnail Image—include a JPG image if desired

STEP 9. Regularly back up your computer's Family Archive folder and its contents to an external device and/or cloud storage service.

STEP 10. Print a copy of your Family Archive Digital Catalog and keep it with the original archive materials.

SAMPLE WORKFLOW FOR LARGE FAMILY ARCHIVE CATALOGS

In a large family archive, material is held in a many archival storage boxes and folders in one or more locations. The digital archive should be stored on an external hard drive because it will be so large. Back up all TIFF digital master copies to a second device. Make digital JPG copies to use for research and projects.

For collections with more than a hundred items, using a unique identification code will greatly expedite your work. It's difficult to organize materials in a family archive if you are working through material one box at a time. Just when you think you've found all the John Smith photos and documents, one more snapshot might turn up and need to be inserted chronologically. It's far easier to separate material by type, and then assign a unique identification code. For example, my family archive includes all the following kinds of items:

Letters (personal and business)

Vital Records

Documents

Newspapers and Newspaper Clippings

Photo Albums and Scrapbooks

Cabinet Card Photographs

Cased Photographs

Black-and-White Snapshots

Oversized Photographs

Color Snapshots

Color Slides

Materials are stored in numerical order in appropriate archival containers—news clippings and newspapers are together, cabinet cards together, snapshots up to 5" × 7" together, oversized photos together, and so on. For simplicity, I use only five record groups—albums, correspondence, vital records, documents, and photographs—but I have added a second letter code to indicate items that are oversized or specialized:

A = album, scrapbook, diary, etc.

L = all letters and correspondence

V = vital records

D = documents, any kind of paper document that isn't a vital record or a letter

DX = oversized document

P = any photograph or snapshot

PX = oversized photograph

PN = photo negative (I have a lot of these)

PS = photo color slide

My unique identification code synchronizes the heirloom original with the digital master copy and points to the storage location. The identification code is followed by a four-digit number, beginning with 0001. All of the zeros are necessary to keep files in order on my computer. Computers always sort by the first digit of a number, instead of the last. So file A1 would end up next to file A10, then it would be A11-19 followed by A100-199 followed by A1000-1999. Then it would be A2 followed by A20-29 followed by A200-299 and so on. Putting the zeros in front keeps files in order from 1 to 9999.

Because my family archive has grown to encompass collections from several family members, I added a three-character archive code to keep each collection separate. Here are sample ID names from the Arline Allen Kinsel Papers (which I code AAK):

AAKA0001 (Album, Photo Album #1)

AAKV0001 (Vital Record, a baptism certificate)

AAKPX0010 (Oversized Photograph, large wedding photo)

AAKDX-0001 (Oversized Document, legal filing for divorce)

AAKD0010 (Document, #10)

Think carefully about the size, scope, and potential additions for your own family archive before you begin cataloging material. Go slowly at first, testing your workflow and making necessary changes. If you have a large collection, it will be a big job, and you'll make steadier progress if you make adjustments to suit your situation.

FAMILY ARCHIVE DIGITAL CATALOG FORM

Item Description	Digital File Name	Location of Original	Keywords	Thumbnail Image

This form is available to download online at <**familytreeuniversity.com/familykeepsakes**>.

FAMILY ARCHIVE DIGITAL CATALOG EXAMPLE

Location Codes: AAK = Arline Allen Kinsel (Archive Name); OD = Oversize Document Box; F = Folder; P = Photo Storage Box; D = Document Box

Item Description	Digital File Name	Location of Original	Keywords	Thumbnail Image
Kinsel/Paulen Marriage Certificate	AAKV0001	AAK, OD1, F1	Kinsel, Paulen, Colorado, Marriage	(optional)
Kinsel, Arline age 18 photo	AAKP0004	AAK, P0012	Arline, Kinsel, Colorado, teen	
Brown, Arline, Santa Ana Public Library Card	AAKD0056	AAK, D4, F3	Brown, Arline, library card	

Workflow

STEP 1. Depending on the number of items in your archive and your overall goals, you may wish to leave the items in the order you established as you set up the original boxes and folders, or reorganize material according to surname, year, or size. Update the original Archive Catalog created in chapter four to reflect any changes.

STEP 2. Create a new folder on your computer hard drive titled *Family Archive Files*.

STEP 3. Inside this folder, create two subfolders: *Archive Digital Master* to hold your TIFF files and *Archive Digital JPG* to hold your JPG files.

STEP 4. Start with one box or folder. As you pick up each item, assign a unique ID code and label each item, either on the archival enclosure or written in pencil on the reverse side of the original document.

An example from my archive is: AAKP0002. This stands for Arline Allen Kinsel Papers Photo 2.

The structure is: Archive Name Abbreviation, Record Group Abbreviation, Item Number.

Note: You may need to scan the front and back of many items; append the small letter *f* (front) or *r* (reverse) to your unique ID code:

AAKP0002f photograph front

AAKP0002r photograph reverse

Use *r* for reverse rather than *b* for back to allow the images to be sorted by your computer with the front side listed first.

STEP 5. Scan each item as a TIFF file and save to the folder named Archive Digital Masters. Use the unique ID code as file names for your digital files to match your Archive Originals.

STEP 6. File the original document numerically with items of the same type. Label boxes or folders if necessary to indicate the contents.

AAKP0001–0076 for photos numbered 01–76

AAKOD for a box of oversized documents

AAKL0124-0270 for letters 124-270

STEP 7. Open the TIFF file, apply keywords and tags if desired. Save the file as a JPG format file to the folder named Archive Digital JPG. Use the exact same name as the TIFF file and let the file extension (.tif or .jpg) differentiate.

STEP 8. Create a new catalog of the digitized items using a word processing table or spreadsheet and save this catalog inside your main Family Archive folder on your computer. See Family Archive Digital Catalog.

Include columns and information for:

Item Description—brief description

Digital File name—your new digital file name

Location of Original—where to find original document or photo

Keywords—names of people, places, events to aid in searches

Thumbnail Image—include a JPG image if desired

STEP 9. Regularly back up your Family Archive folder and its contents to an external device and/or cloud storage service.

STEP 10. Print a catalog listing of the contents of your family archive and keep it with the original archive materials.

TIFF ARCHIVE

Museums and archives recommend using the TIFF format when archiving historic documents because it is a lossless format that does not compress files. This is great for archiving images where the aim is to preserve all information in the original, but it will also result in extremely large file sizes.

If you are archiving one-of-a-kind documents and photographs, consider scanning and saving in TIFF format. Each time a JPG document is opened, edited, and saved, the image loses quality from compression. Changes may not be noticeable in the first few versions, but continued degradation can severely affect the quality of your image.

If you can't use TIFF, store one untouched JPG file as your archive document, and use a copy for editing, saving, and resizing. Never touch your archived JPG.

While TIFF is a great format for archiving documents, the file size can be a disadvantage. Photo sharing sites, genealogy database programs, websites, and e-publishing all prefer JPG format images. You will need to convert your archived TIFF files to JPG format in order to use the files for other purposes. Many photo-organizing software programs, both free and commercial, will easily convert files.

This sample workflow for working with a birth certificate held in your family archive adds TIFF to JPG conversion when working with your archived documents.

STEP 1. Scan the original paper certificate in TIFF format.

STEP 2. Return the original to archival storage.

STEP 3. Name your digital image according to your chosen file-naming scheme. Save this archive TIFF file on an external storage device.

STEP 4. Convert the TIFF file to JPG format, maintaining the original file name with the JPG file extension. This is your working copy. Use this copy to make duplicates for editing, sharing, and Web projects.

STEP 5. Open your working digital JPG copy and your genealogy database or a word processing document. Transcribe the information from the birth certificate. If you are using a word processing document, save this digital transcription using the original file name and adding the code *tr* for transcription. If you are transcribing within your genealogy database software, the information will be included in your database.

Congratulations! Your original document now exists in four different forms and three digital versions:

1. The original archived document
2. The archived TIFF version
3. The working copy JPG version
4. The transcribed version in a word-processing file or in your genealogy database

JPG ARCHIVE

For various reasons, some researchers prefer to work with JPG format files. JPG is a lossy format, so over time, as the file is open and modified, the quality of the file will diminish. You can minimize photo degradation by using one JPG copy as your Archive Master Copy, and other copies for research and projects.

When you scan an archive original document, file one untouched JPG file as your Digital Master Copy. Name your digital image according to your chosen file-naming scheme, adding the code *arc* for archive at the end of the file name. Save this archive JPG file on an external storage device. Never alter the archive JPG copy. Create a duplicate JPG copy for editing, saving, and resizing.

The workflow for digitizing an archive original document for a JPG archive is the same as the TIFF archive.

WORKING WITH YOUR DIGITAL ARCHIVE FILES

After you've digitized your family archive collection, what's next? With TIFF Digital Master Copies securely stored in multiple locations (Think: Lots Of Copies Keeps Stuff Safe, or LOCKSS), you are ready to extract information, edit photos, create books and other projects, and share your collection.

The computer software you choose for these tasks is limited only by your need and expertise. Remember to always preserve your master TIFF copies and work with JPG files whether you are transcribing letters between sweethearts, editing a wedding photo, or creating a collage of old family homes.

As you investigate software solutions for your family history research and creative projects, don't ignore Web-based solutions and mobile apps. Many times, these programs fill a specialized need and trade lots of bells and whistles for low cost and ease of use.

RESOURCES

Viewing and Transcribing Documents

TRANSCRIPT 2.3 (PC) by Jacob Boerema **<www.jacobboerema.nl/en>**. A handy program that opens an image file and text file together for easier transcription of handwritten documents. Features allow users to magnify, increase contrast, and clarify images.

Working With Images

ADOBE LIGHTROOM (PC, Mac) **<www.adobe.com>** is the photo organizer of choice for professional photographers and can easily handle batch file naming and image conversion.

ADOBE PHOTOSHOP ELEMENTS (PC, Mac) **<www.adobe.com>** is a photo editor and organizer with keyword, tagging, and editing capabilities. Features easy social-media sharing, creative projects, and albums. Converts JPG / TIFF files.

APPLE IPHOTO (Mac) **<www.apple.com>** is a photo organizer and editor and is tightly integrated with Mac and iOS products.

FLICKR <www.flickr.com> is used by the Library of Congress and countless institutions to share public domain photos with the public. Private and copyright settings allow more control for users as well.

GOOGLE PICASA <picasa.google.com> is one of the most popular Web-based photo programs, allowing you to organize, edit, and share your photos easily and from any computer.

XNVIEW (PC, Linux, Mac, iPad) **<www.xnview.com>** and **XNVIEW CONVERT** (Win, Linux, Mac) **<www.xnconvert.com>** is a cross-platform image viewer, batch image converter, and resizer that supports all common picture and graphic formats. This free software is great for converting JPG / TIFF to create archive files.

Information Management

Do you have lots of little notes you'd like to organize and access for research or future reference? These outstanding solutions in information management are even better than a full-time file clerk.

BENTO (Mac, iOS) **<www.filemaker.com/products/bento>** is a database software program that can be customized for a variety of projects from note-taking to source lists to research logs. A library of user templates offers even more custom solutions.

DEVONTHINK (Mac) **<www.devontechnologies.com>** is a popular choice for researchers, business professionals, and anyone who needs to work with information. One of DEVONthink's most unique features is the "artificial intelligence" that suggests tags and groups based on content. DEVONthink comes in multiple versions from simple to full-featured.

EVERNOTE (Web, PC, Mac, mobile) **<www.evernote.com>** is a powerful, yet simple, idea. Drop any file into Evernote and it becomes searchable on text and tags. Snap a photo with your mobile phone, e-mail it to Evernote, and tag it to appear with other images. Organize genealogy notes by surname or just search for information as needed.

FILEMAKER (PC, Mac, Web) **<www.filemaker.com>** is the big brother edition of Bento and is a powerful database software popular in business and education.

PAPERLESS (PC, Mac) **<www.marinersoftware.com>** software organizes scanned notes and documents into a digital filing system. The built-in OCR makes files searchable and easy to find.

11

Organize Your Paper Files

If you've spent time searching for papers instead of searching for ancestors, you know the value of an organized filing system. In genealogy research, paper piles seem to grow faster than new twigs on the family tree. Abstracts, birth registrations, census reports—it's an alphabet soup of genealogy records, and the only way to control the chaos is with a paper plan that suits you and your research.

Computer-minded researchers tend to look for ways to integrate their paper and digital file systems while veteran researchers, with research going back for decades, may use a paper-centered approach. Beginning genealogists often set up elaborate systems and then look for ways to streamline their filing time.

A lot of researchers think they need a new or better system, when all that's really needed is a daily filing method. Where is your biggest frustration: your file storage, your filing system, or your daily filing routine? This chapter addresses each of these key areas and will help you create a filing system that fits your style and meets your needs. Resources offer links to tutorials and further information.

FIVE FACTS FOR FILING SUCCESS

1. THE PERFECT FILING SYSTEM DOES NOT EXIST. What's perfect for one researcher might be too simple or too complicated for you. Look for a filing method that suits your level of expertise, your time, and your style. A beginning researcher needs a simple program that can expand as papers multiply; a weekend worker may need something efficient and intuitive to accommodate long breaks between research blocks.

2. A FILING SYSTEM IS NOT FOREVER. If your system isn't working, fix it, or try a different method. Recognize that the method advocated by your best genealogy buddy just isn't working for you. First, try to tweak your routine and see if you can adapt it to better suit your needs. If not, spend some time thinking about what might work better for you and then move on to a different system.

3. TEST DRIVE BEFORE YOU BUY. Most genealogists have tried a few different filing schemes throughout their career. Some find that a combination of systems works best, or they develop a unique filing arrangement that answers their needs. Save yourself time and trouble by thoroughly testing any new-to-you filing routine before moving all your papers from folders to binders or vice versa. Put a new program through its paces with your current project, or move over one surname or family group. If the new system suits you better, then gradually move over everything, one project, one surname at a time.

4. SUCCESS DEPENDS ON PRACTICE. Any filing system is only as good as the papers you put into it. You have to use it to make it work. If it's complicated or time-consuming, you may continue to pile rather than file your papers. If your method is overly simple, such as too few folders for the quantity of papers stored, you may find it impossible to retrieve files or find papers within them. Set up your filing system and commit yourself to faithfully using it for three or six months. Use it, tweak it, and make it your own before you give up and try another one. A successful routine builds on understanding your own research style combined with practice, practice, practice.

5. FILE AND SMILE. Your final filing solution should make you smile. It should be as easy to locate your copy of your fourth-great-grandmother's birth record as it is to find yesterday's transcription of the 1920 census.

Strategies to Tame the Paper Tiger

Effective file management for the twenty-first century genealogist needs to do more than just store papers. A successful system also needs to:

- ☐ be logical and intuitive to set up
- ☐ make it easy to *file* documents
- ☐ make it easy to *find* documents
- ☐ play well with other formats—digital, paper printouts, and archived heirloom originals
- ☐ grow with expanding research

SELECT YOUR FILE STORAGE METHOD

The first step in effectively organizing your files is to decide where and how you want to store your files. Your storage solution will depend the on space available and your own personal preferences. Sit back and take a deep breath. Clear your mind of the frustrations and piles of files. Close your eyes and imagine your ideal genealogy workspace. Are you looking at a file cabinet, a bookcase of nicely labeled binders, or a computer with a scanner and a backup drive?

Your answer to this question should give you some idea of how to proceed. Some people like to work with vertical files and folders that can be easily moved, relabeled, and then tucked out of sight. Others like the three-ring binder approach with files that don't get shuffled or misfiled. Still others want to go paperless and dream of a digital office.

Combine this vision of your ideal workspace with the pros and cons of the alternatives to help you decide what kind of storage system will work best for you.

Vertical File Folders

ADVANTAGES
- easy to move and reorganize
- inexpensive
- easily available
- expandable
- files can be pulled out for specific projects

DISADVANTAGES
- easily misfiled or misplaced
- items inside can become shuffled
- file folder labels can fall off

CONSIDERATIONS
- colored folders or labels can help keep files organized
- hanging file folders can help organize folders
- sheet protectors add to cost
- choice of filing cabinet, file boxes, or portable plastic file bins

SUPPLIES NEEDED
- filing cabinet, file box, or bin
- manila office file folders, three cut
- file folder labels, white permanent
- hanging file folders to group manila folders (optional)
- plastic label tabs for hanging file folders (optional)

Binders

ADVANTAGES

- documents less likely to become lost
- papers can be arranged in a specific way
- easy to pull out and examine entire contents
- may be more easily shared with others

DISADVANTAGES

- more expensive than folders
- require shelf space
- require tab dividers for organization
- can become heavy and unwieldy

CONSIDERATIONS

- sheet protectors add to bulk and weight
- sheet protectors add to cost
- hole punching or sheet protectors add extra step to filing

SUPPLIES NEEDED

- 2-inch, three-ring binders, plastic view cover is helpful
- extra-wide tab dividers, eight per set work well
- office quality sheet protectors

Digital File Storage

ADVANTAGES

- green solution—less paper, ink, waste
- mobile
- saves space
- easy retrieval for sharing
- saves cost of paper and filing supplies

DISADVANTAGES

- requires scanner, backup program
- no archival hard copies
- information only accessible via technology

CONSIDERATIONS

- need to update file media regularly
- need access plan for heirs

Remember the first fact for filing success: The perfect filing system does not exist. You may not be 100 percent satisfied with a system of file folders, binders, or digital files, but choose the one that seems most likely to work for you. As you become more comfortable with your overall file storage system, you may decide to adapt a different method for a specific project. This is a great way to maximize efficiency.

Combining Methods

You aren't limited to choosing only one of these styles. You may find you prefer a combination of these systems. Some possible ways to combine styles are:

- Use vertical file folders for your overall system and binders for one-name studies.
- Use vertical file folders for your overall system and binders for lineage data.
- Use binders for your overall system and file folders for research logs and locality documents.
- Use binders for your overall system and digital files for reports and analysis.
- Use digital files for a paperless system, except for one set of paper files for your direct line.

Archival vs. Office Supply

There's a big difference in cost and availability for archival vs. office-quality filing supplies. For general research filing, it's not necessary to use archival supplies. Instead, recycle old office folders and binders or shop for special offers at your local office supply store.

CATEGORIZE YOUR FILES

After you've selected a file storage method, consider how you will organize the files within that system. There's no standard filing protocol, as there would be if you were setting up files for a doctor's office, and that's okay. Use what works for you.

Genealogists need to manage several kinds of information in many different formats—from paper to digital. Overall, your genealogical files can be categorized in one of two categories:

1. PEOPLE AND SOURCES—information that ties generations together; the documents that support your family lines.

2. RESEARCH SUPPORT DOCUMENTS—information that helps you put together the material in number one; that is, repository information, how-to notes, state and county research guides, research logs, research trips, conference and workshop notes.

It's helpful to set up separate filing systems for each category. You'll find you use your research support documents for all of your research while you'll access people and source files more selectively as you work on an individual ancestor or surname.

Genealogy file systems are as varied as the genealogists who create them. The best system is the one that suits the work style, personality, and time of the researcher.

COMMON GENEALOGY FILING SYSTEMS

Genealogy research is all about people, so filing information according to individuals might seem like a logical solution. Within only a few generations, however, the number of names quickly multiplies, and before long, you may be labeling folders or tabs for thousands of names.

In addition, many sources include information about more than one person. Each vital record may include information about the individual, his spouse, his parents, and even his children. If your paper filing system involves placing all source material in a folder or binder organized by individual, you will need to photocopy the document and place copies with each person, or cross-reference the document at another location.

It quickly becomes obvious that some systems require more file folders, binders, dividers, and paper copies than other systems. Some researchers have found ways to minimize duplication by using a source-based system that cross-references source records.

Storing Heirloom Documents

You may be wondering how your heirloom documents fit within a genealogy filing system, and the answer is: they don't. Please do not keep your precious family papers mixed in with computer printouts and research logs.

Everyday research files are subject to the all of the following hazards. Protect your heirloom documents from:

- exposure to light, dust, and temperature and humidity fluctuations
- spilled food and drink
- frequent handling
- loss due to misfiling
- damage in a natural disaster
- becoming orphaned when you're gone

Instead, place a photocopy of the original document in your files and store the heirloom original in appropriate archival containers.

The following four genealogy filing systems are among the most popular with genealogists with all levels of experience. Look for websites containing more information in the Resources section at the end of this chapter.

File by Individual

Files are arranged by surname/individual. This system arranges material according to individuals by name; women are labeled by their maiden name.

FOR FILE FOLDERS

1. Label a file drawer section with a surname.
2. Label folders with names of individuals: surname, first name, and birthdate (b. 1824).
3. Arrange folders alphabetically behind each surname.
4. File records for each individual inside file folders.
    a. Arrange in chronological order.
    b. File records concerning more than one person (marriage, census) with the husband or head of family and cross-reference to other individuals with a photocopy or notation.

FOR THREE-RING BINDERS

1. Label a binder or binder section with a surname.
2. Label tab dividers with names of individuals: surname, first name, and birthdate (b. 1824).
3. Arrange tab dividers alphabetically behind each surname.
4. File records for each individual behind tab dividers.
   a. Arrange in chronological order.
   b. File records concerning more than one person (marriage, census) with the husband or head of family and cross-reference to other individuals with a photocopy or notation.

Record Identification Numbers

Many genealogy database programs automatically assign unique numbers to individuals and to and couples:

- RIN (Record Identification Number) is a unique number for each individual
- MRIN (Marriage Record Identification Number) is a unique number for each couple

ADVANTAGES

- easy to set up and maintain
- easy to expand
- can be synchronized with genealogy software, archive material, and digital files arranged by individual name
- easy to share material on individuals
- good for single-person studies
- easy to understand
- can provide a full picture of the person

DISADVANTAGES

- individual files require many tabs or folders
- can require more physical storage space in file cabinets or binders
- more difficult to "see" family groups
- requires use of photocopies or cross-references

CONSIDERATIONS

- can be synchronized with Record Identification Number (RIN) in genealogy database program
- Table of Contents or File List can help keep track of documents for each person

File by Couple or Family Group

Files are arranged by Surname/Couple or Surname/Family Group. This system arranges material according to families and is labeled by the names of husband and wife. Unmarried individuals are filed with parents until they marry.

FOR FILE FOLDERS

1. Label a file drawer section with a surname.
2. Label folders with names of couples: surname, first name of husband and first name, maiden name of wife.
3. Arrange folders alphabetically behind each surname.
4. File records for each family group inside file folders.
    a. Arrange in chronological order.
    b. File records concerning more than one family (probate, census) with head of family and cross-reference to other families with a photocopy or notation.

FOR THREE-RING BINDERS

1. Label a binder or binder section with a surname.
2. Label tab dividers with names of couples: surname, first name of husband and first name, maiden name of wife.
3. Arrange tab dividers alphabetically behind each surname.
4. File records for each family group behind dividers.
    a. Arrange in chronological order.
    b. File records concerning more than one family (probate, census) with head of family and cross reference to other families with a photocopy or notation.

ADVANTAGES

- fewer file folders or tab dividers than individual system
- easy to set up and maintain
- easy to expand
- can be synchronized with genealogy software, archive material, and digital files arranged by family group
- files can be color-coded by family line for easier access
- easy to share material on one family group or family line
- easy to understand
- can provide a full picture of the couple
- Family Group Sheet or File List can be used as Table of Contents for records in each file

DISADVANTAGES

- requires photocopies or cross-references to some source documents
- unmarried individuals remain with parents, which can make them more difficult to find

CONSIDERATIONS

- can be synchronized with Marriage Record Identification Number (MRIN) in genealogy database program
- can be adapted for use with pedigree numbering (see File by Person Number)

File by Person Number

Files can also be arranged by a software-assigned reference number. Many genealogy database programs such as Legacy Family Tree, RootsMagic, and Reunion automatically assign individual or family identification numbers. This filing system arranges material by an assigned number, and has the distinct advantage of easy expansion without the need for refiling. The setup for either file folders or three-ring binders is essentially the same.

1. Each individual or couple is assigned a sequential number. Some software programs assign a Record Identification Number (RIN) or Marriage Record Identification Number (MRIN).
2. A Table of Contents listing all numbers and corresponding names or family groups is placed at the beginning of the file or notebook.
3. File folders or tabbed dividers are labeled with the Record Number.
4. All documents for the individual or family group are filed behind the number.
5. If you are using the MRIN, unmarried individuals remain with the family group until they are married.
6. Use photocopies or cross-reference source documents that include more than one individual or family group, depending on your chosen system.

ADVANTAGES

- easy to set up and maintain
- easy to expand
- synchronizes easily with genealogy software RIN or MRIN numbers
- Family Group Sheet can be used as Table of Contents for records in each file
- easy to share material as grouped

DISADVANTAGES

- requires photocopies or cross-references to some source documents
- needs Table of Contents to locate people
- not easy to share material on one family group or family line with others
- more difficult to synchronize with archive material stored by name

CUSTOM REFERENCE NUMBERS

Set up your system using a custom Reference Number, instead of the software assigned Marriage Record Identification Number (MRIN) or Record Identification Number (RIN), for either individuals or family groups. This allows you to add a code for Surname or Family Line code. Some researchers use a number devised from the pedigree chart.

This method also ensures that your Reference Number will transfer with a GEDCOM file between software programs.

FOR A CUSTOM SURNAME/FAMILY LINE SYSTEM

1. Divide files into your four family lines:

paternal grandfather

paternal grandmother

maternal grandfather

maternal grandmother

2. Give each line a one or two letter abbreviation: S for Smith, or Ha for Harris, Hi for Higgins.

3. Keep a master list for each line and add numbers consecutively as you add new couples/ family groups to the file system:

Ha1009—John Harris and Susan Mitchell

Ha1010—James Harris and Mary Smith

ADVANTAGES

- easy to set up and maintain
- easy to expand
- can be synchronized with genealogy software, archive material, and digital files arranged by surname
- can be color-coded by family line for easier access
- easy to share material on one family group or family line

DISADVANTAGES

- requires photocopies or cross-references to some source documents
- needs Table of Contents to locate people

File by Source Number

Another organizational system focuses on filing paper copies of source documentation and cross-referencing documents to people, rather than filing the sources along with the individual or family files. This system is popular with researchers who prefer to minimize duplication and excess paper and works especially well when organized through a computer database or spreadsheet.

The Source Number System focuses on organizing sources and cross-referencing the source record to names and families. All sources are given a unique number and filed sequentially in vertical files or binders. This number can be assigned to one or several individuals or families without the need to photocopy records.

The set up for vertical files or binders is essentially the same:

1. Assign a four- or five-digit number to the first source document and write the number in the upper right-hand corner of the paper.

2. List number and document type on a Table of Contents sheet at the front of the file (or keep on your computer).

3. Continue to add new source documents sequentially.

4. File documents in file folders or binders sequentially.

5. Add tab dividers or file folders to hold groups of ten to twenty-five documents.

6. Cross-reference documents by assigned number to individuals and families in paper notes and genealogy software.

VARIATIONS

1. Use abbreviations for Surnames or Family Lines to divide the source documents into smaller groups. With this method, all documents for one family are filed as they are acquired and not divided into record groups. For example:

    Smith Family includes:

    Sm0001—birth record for Michael Smith, b. 1827

    Sm0002—1850 census for Michael Smith Family

    Sm0003—probate record and transcription for Michael Smith, 1827-1859

    Harris Line includes:

    Ha0016—divorce record for Henry and Rhoda Harris, 1976

    Ha0017—birth record for Percy Harris, b. 1790

    Ha0018—1930 census for Harold Harris Family

2. Keep census records separate from other family documents. These records are readily available online. You may choose to print out only selected records for your files.

    Census Records:

    C0001—1930 census for Harold Harris Family

    C0002—1850 census for Michael Smith Family

    C0003—1885 state census for Henry R. Harris Family

3. Instead of creating Surname or Family Line groups, create four or five larger Record Groups that hold all records within that group.

    Vitals includes:

    V0001—birth record for Michael Smith, b. 1827

    V0002—divorce record for Henry and Rhoda Harris, 1976

    V0003—birth record for Percy Harris, b. 1790

    Census includes:

    C0001—1930 census for Harold Harris Family

    C0002—1850 census for Michael Smith Family

    C0003—1885 state census for Henry R. Harris Family

Common record groups for this system include:

Vital Records

Census

Military

Directories

Newspapers

Legal and Property

Be wary of using too many record groups and forcing decisions, such as where to file a probate record: legal or property?

ADVANTAGES

- eliminates need for duplicate copies of source documentation
- saves filing space, paper, copying, and filing time
- easy to set-up and maintain
- easy to expand
- can be synchronized with genealogy software, archive material, and digital files arranged numerically
- can be color-coded by family line for easier access
- easy to share material on one family group or family line
- easy to understand
- can provide a full picture of the couple
- Family Group Sheet or File List can be used as Table of Contents for records in each file

DISADVANTAGES

- requires cross-referencing.
- more difficult to pull documentation for an individual or family because sources may be scattered throughout the files
- requires maintaining an up-to-date Table of Contents

More Filing Ideas

Genealogy filing systems are as unique as the researchers who create and use them. Here are more ideas from veteran genealogists:

- File everything about a family within that family file, from research logs and correspondence to county maps and birth certificates. Duplicate copies are used to eliminate the need for cross-referencing.
- Use a filing system that synchronizes with your genealogy database, such as the Marriage Record Identification Number (MRIN) filing method taught by genealogist Karen Clifford (see the Resources section at the end of this chapter).
- File census records in a separate folder or tab, marked with the surname and county to minimize the need for multiple copies. These records are cross-referenced in the genealogy database software and on Family Group Sheet sources.
- Create a "Coffee Table Book" that can be enjoyed by browsers and researchers in a system popularized by Pat Richley-Erickson, a.k.a. DearMYRTLE, in workshops and her Monthly Organization Checklist (see the Resources section at the end of this chapter).
- Use locality folders or binders to contain all or additional records from a specific county or region. This helps to consolidate records of the same type and minimize the need for duplicate copies.

- Use color-coding to differentiate family lines, such as used in the system taught by Mary Hill (see the Resources section at the end of this chapter).

See the Resources section of this chapter for links to webinars and tutorials on this subject.

ESTABLISH A DAILY FILING ROUTINE

The method you choose to organize your paper files will only be effective when you use it regularly and efficiently. If you have to refer to your filing guide every time you need to file or find a piece of paper, you will quickly become frustrated and abandon filing altogether. Likewise, if you need to rely on a hole punch that is in the other room, or have run out of sheet protectors, you will find it easier to pile instead of file your work at the end of the day.

Behavioral research tells us that it takes twenty-one days to make a new habit. Begin with your next research day and commit twenty-one days to your new filing system. Each day, close up your office with a routine that ends by putting away all the paper you have accumulated throughout the day.

Curator's Filing Tips

If you are new to genealogy:
- Start slow.
- Let it grow with you.
- If something isn't working, stop and figure out why. Tweak it.

If you want a fresh start:
- Work from the present forward.
- Incorporate old files as you have time.
- Start with current research.
- Don't attempt to reorganize your entire filing system at once.

FILE FIRST: DAILY CHECKLIST

You Need

- ☐ small-size sticky notes
- ☐ file folder labels or tab inserts
- ☐ a supply of file folders, tab dividers, and sheet protectors for your system
- ☐ a desktop "To Be Filed" box or folder to hold papers accumulated throughout the day that will need to be filed
- ☐ personal scanner for scanning nonessential paper copies

Your Routine

- Start the day with a filing warm-up. Put away anything left from the previous research day before starting fresh.
- Keep a supply of small sticky notes on the desktop.
- Keep letter-size paper, file folders, tab dividers, and sheet protectors within easy reach.

- All paper is standard 8½" × 11" in size. Photocopy or scan random-sized notes to standard-sized paper.
- As you work, label papers *To File* or *To Scan* with a sticky note naming the file location and place paper in a desktop box.
- Don't stop and file papers individually.
- Keep folders for current projects in a handy file box or drawer.
- Take a filing break midday or about fifteen minutes before ending your research day.
- When you return from a research trip, file papers first.
- End the day with a filing cool down. Don't leave the office until you file your papers.

What to Do When Life Happens

When you run late and have to choose between filing papers or starting dinner, keep your family happy and leave filing for the next day. The next time you research, file any papers left out from your previous research session before you get to work.

Filing my most recent work is a good warm-up and reminder of what I was doing. By the time I am finished with the paperwork, I am already engrossed in my project and well on my way for the day.

USE A PERSONAL FILE GUIDE

The final step in setting up your filing system is to make your own personal File Guide.

Anyone who might need to use your work in the future will be able to understand your system—including you!

For many years, my genealogy time was carefully carved out of long weekends and summer vacations. Each time I pulled out my files after a long hiatus, it seemed like I had to spend time reacquainting myself with my filing rules and how-tos. Finally, I typed up a simple File Guide and placed a copy at the front of my main research binder. It was one of the best timesavers I've ever found.

Your File Guide (see an example at the end of this chapter) will be different from mine, but should include an overview of your organizational system and a simple listing of the rules you file by.

RESOURCES

Genealogy Database Software

PC

Family Tree Maker **<www.ancestry.com>**
Legacy Family Tree **<www.legacyfamilytree.com>**
RootsMagic **<www.rootsmagic.com>**

Notebook Filing Conventions—Keep It Simple

To Find Records on an Individual or a Couple

1. Use the Alpha Index.
2. Find the person's Surname and Marriage Record Identification Number (MRIN).
3. Unmarried individuals are filed behind the MRIN of their parents.

Numbered Tabs

1. Individuals and couples are filed behind their MRIN tab.
2. Unmarried individuals are filed behind their parents' MRIN.
3. Individuals with multiple marriages are filed with the direct-line MRIN.
4. Spouses and nondirect line individuals from a multiple marriage are filed with the MRIN for that marriage.
   a. Example: Arline Kinsel and Charles Parker—Arline married Charles but had no children by him and then went on to marry Frank Brown, the direct-line ancestor; the Kinsel/Parker MRIN tab holds information on the Kinsel/Parker marriage and for Charles Parker. Other information on Arline has been moved forward to the Arline Kinsel/Frank Brown MRIN.

Surname, Locality, Subject Tabs

Documents for more than one family group are filed under the Surname or Subject Tab, except:
   1. Census records are filed with Head of Household.
   2. Local history documents are filed by State: County: Locality.
   3. Unidentified "persons of interest" are filed under AWOL.
   4. Neighbors, etc., are filed by Surname: Locality: Neighbors.

MAC

Family Tree Maker **<www.ancestry.com>**

MacFamilyTree **<www.syniumsoftware.com/macfamilytree>**

Reunion **<www.leisterpro.com>**

Genealogy File Organization Systems

Conquering the Paper Monster, by Elyse Doerflinger (e-book)

FamilyRoots Organizer, by Mary Hill **<www.familyrootsorganizer.com>**

Organize Your Paper Files, by Karen Clifford **<www.fileyourpapers.com>**

Monthly Organization Checklist, by DearMYRTLE, Pat Richley-Erickson **<www.dearmyrtle.com>**

Webinars and Workshops

"Organization Made Easy: 5 Simple Ways to Get Your Family History in Order," *Family Tree Magazine* Webinars **<www.shopfamilytree.com/product/445>**

Genea Webinars **<www.blog.geneawebinars.com>**

Legacy Family Tree Webinars **<www.legacyfamilytree.com/webinars.asp>**

12

Organize Your Computer

Does your computer desktop resemble your real office desk? Is it covered with digital folders and files? For those of us who grew up with note cards and file cabinets, the urge to save multiple copies of documents can be a habit hard to break, and we may be doing the same thing on our computer desktops that we do at our physical desks. How many digital copies do you really need to keep?

Computers are great for processing information and filing and archiving stuff, but to efficiently store and retrieve information, you have to play by the rules. The good news is there are only four steps to an organized computer hard drive:

1. Purge old files.
2. Use a consistent file-naming system.
3. Use a simple folder structure.
4. Back up your hard drive.

In this chapter, we'll work through each step to help you become a more efficient and effective computer user. Resources will point you to software and hardware solutions.

PURGE OLD FILES

The first step toward an organized computer is to purge your old files. Start by cleaning up your computer desktop, then work your way through your loose documents, reestablishing order with your digital files. Use this checklist as a reminder to help you master the chaos:

☐ Tidy your computer desktop by deleting multiple copies of old documents and random files.

☐ Delete unused alias files.

☐ Open your Downloads or Temporary files folder and move files you've saved somewhere else to the Trash.

☐ Check your Applications folder and remove applications you no longer need or want.

☐ Open your Documents folder and locate any loose files. Move to the proper subfolder or delete unneeded files.

☐ Empty the Trash regularly.

Empty the Trash

Deleting files only moves files to the Trash or Recycle Bin on your computer. The Trash has to be emptied for the files to be permanently deleted. On a PC or Mac, right-click the Recycle Bin or Trash icon and select Empty Recycle Bin or Empty Trash.

USE A CONSISTENT FILE-NAMING SCHEME

As you tidy your desktop, and organize your computer folders, take time to consistently name any unnamed or new files. Don't feel like you need to rename everything right now, but make it a habit as you go forward to consistently use a naming scheme that is easy to remember. The following file-naming conventions are commonly recommended by document records agencies:

AVOID SPECIAL CHARACTERS IN A FILE NAME: \ / | [ ] { } < > : ; * % , @ #

USE UNDERSCORES AND DASHES INSTEAD OF PERIODS AND SPACES. Punctuation and spaces have a special purpose when used in a file name. Periods tell the computer program where the file extension begins. Spaces are interpreted as *%20*. For example, the file name *turner marriage.doc* will appear online as *turner%20marriage.doc*. Preserve the meaning of your file names by avoiding punctuation and using the underscore and dash characters in place of spaces.

KEEP FILE NAMES SHORT. Some operating systems limit the length of file names; the URL will be included, making the total file name longer. Use consistent abbreviations if necessary to keep file names short. Use standard two-letter abbreviations for states and months. Develop your own surname and name abbreviations if your family names are lengthy, but remember to use these abbreviations consistently.

NAME FILES TO STAND ALONE. Files are frequently copied and moved to other folders, or transferred between users and systems. Give your files a name that will stand alone without relying on a folder name for meaning. For example: *turner-susan_marriage_1962.doc* is a better file name than: *susan_marriage_1962.doc* (filed within a Turner folder).

The second file name is fine as long as the file remains within the Turner folder, but when it is removed from the folder, it might be confused with other similar files from other folders.

FORMAT DATES CONSISTENTLY. Whether you place dates at the beginning or end of the file name, use a consistent format. YYYY_MM_DD or YYYYMMDD. YYYY is the year; MM the two-digit abbreviation for the month; DD the two-digit abbreviation for the date. Using this order allows the file to be sorted chronologically in year, month, date order.

MANAGE MULTIPLE VERSIONS WITH VERSION NUMBERS FOR CHANGING DOCUMENTS.

For notes and documents that go through various versions, use the letter *v* to represent *version number* and add a two-digit number, *v01*, *v02*, etc.

This allows the file name to remain the same and keep all versions together and sorted numerically. Avoid using words like *old*, *new*, *revised*, etc. The exception is using the word *final* to indicate the last and final version of a document; use the word singly without a version number to easily locate the file.

USE STANDARD FILE EXTENSIONS FOR MULTIPLE COPIES OF A FILE. This is especially helpful with image files that require different formats for different uses. It is important to keep the same base file name so that the files remain together in sorting and searching. Allow the file extension to help you differentiate between files.

The scanned image of an archive document may be named: *kinsel-arline_1906_teen.TIFF*. When this file is converted to a JPG image for use in a digital album, it can be named: *kinsel-arline_1906_teen.JPG*. The same file, reduced in size for a Web page or edited for a blog post, can be named: *kinsel-arline_1906_teen_web.JPG*; *kinsel-arline_1906_teen_web-edit.JPG*. By appending any necessary information at the end of the file name, the files will remain together as a group.

BE CONSISTENT. Whatever file-naming scheme you choose, stick with it.

Create a File-Naming Cheat Sheet

My file-naming scheme has four parts, each separated by an underscore, plus the file extension; I use a dash to separate words within each part: name_date_place_item.file extension or surname-firstname_yyyymmdd_state-place_item.ext.

1. Name with surname first: surname-first name or initial
2. Date in year month day format: yyyymmdd
3. Place with location listed from largest to smallest: state two-letter abbreviation-county-town
4. Item: short item description

For example: *kinsel-arline_19021030_co-pueblo_play-cast.jpg*.

My preference is to use all lowercase characters. I add version information at the end of the file name to help identify different kinds of files, for example, this is the file name for the Web image: *kinsel-arline_19021030_co-pueblo_play-cast_web.jpg*.

FILE-NAMING CHEAT SHEET

When I first started working with my grandmother's archives, my scanning time came in bits and pieces often separated by weeks or months. I had a hard time remembering my file-naming scheme until I made a simple one-page poster and tacked it above my computer.

Source Document File Names

name_date_place_item.file extension

surname-firstname_yyyymmdd_state-place_item.ext

example: *kinsel-arline_19021030_co-pueblo_play-cast.jpg*

example: *kinsel-eb_1920uscensus_ks-atchison-grasshopper.pdf*

Research Document File Names

subject name_item.doc

example: *kinsel-arline_research-notes.doc*

General Genealogy Document File Names

subject_item.file extension

example: *ngs2010_research-plan-lecture.doc*

example: *ngs2013_syllabus.pdf*

I try to keep file names short and consistent, and use all lowercase letters. I also use underscore and dash characters in place of spaces. The file extension tells me if it is a photo, PDF, movie, or document.

This scheme is extended to working documents by exchanging the date and identification for a document title: *kinsel-arline_research-notes.doc.* For more general documents, use a similar name and title scheme: *ngs2013_research-plan-lecture.doc.* Add revision numbers as necessary to track changes and updates to your work.

Use a file-naming scheme that works for you, and remember to be consistent.

USE A SIMPLE FOLDER STRUCTURE

Organizing computer files and folders doesn't have to be confusing or complicated. I've found that the old scout motto "Keep It Super Simple" is generally good advice when it comes to organizing most anything, especially computer files.

Software designers know how people work, which is why they design several folders as part of the structure of your operating system. Whether you use a PC or a Mac, start by using the folders already set up on your hard drive: Documents, Movies, Pictures, Music. Keep things tidy by dropping new files inside the appropriate folder for easier backups and faster searching.

Create subfolders inside your main folders to further organize your projects. Here are a few ideas to get you started with your genealogy files:

- In the Documents folder, create subfolders for broad categories: Home, Business, Genealogy, Blogs, Volunteer.
- Keep all genealogy-related documents together in your Genealogy folder within your Documents folder. It's easy to copy this entire folder to a USB flash drive to take your research with you, to copy the data for a cousin, or to back up the information for security.

Tip

Fewer folders mean fewer places to look, and fewer steps when saving other computer files.

- Within your Genealogy folder, create more nested folders, either by surname, place name, or record group.
- Take advantage of your computer's skill in sorting and searching; avoid the temptation to make lots of folders containing a few files each. Your computer can easily search inside a folder, whether it contains ten files or ten thousand.
- Use consistent file naming to group items and make them easy to find.
- Do *not* rely on folder names for file identification. Files are often removed from folders and need individual names that include surnames, states, counties, etc.

Sample Folder Structure

I like to keep things simple and lean, and use my computer searching ability when I want to find files. Here's a peek inside my Genealogy folder, located inside my main Documents folder:

Genealogy
    Correspondence
    Database Files
    Gen Finance
    Gen Projects
    Military
    Places
    Research Resources
    Surnames
        Brown
        Chamblin
        Child
        Kinsel
            Kinsel Notes
            Kinsel Bible
            kinsel-arline_1902_school.jpg
            kinsel-eb_1900_mo-jackson_census.pdf
            kinsel-eb_1920_ks-johnson_census.jpg

Levenick

Mathewson

Files about specific surnames are placed inside the family surname folder; the computer sorts and groups names together. Subfolders help group many documents related to a particular record. For example: In my Kinsel surname folder, two subfolders hold relevant files: Kinsel Bible record pages and Kinsel Notes for research notes, timelines, and transcriptions.

I can quickly scan the computer file listing to find other records, such as census files or school photos, without tedious searching through nested folders. Fewer folders means fewer places to look, and fewer steps when saving other computer files.

Find Files Fast

Your computer filing system, like your paper filing system, is only successful if you can find the files you store. Fortunately, performing custom searches is one of the tasks that computers do best. Both PC and Mac operating systems include a built-in search feature; learn to use it and start saving time now. Microsoft Windows XP and Windows 7 Users can use Search <www.support.microsoft.com>. Mac Users can use Spotlight and the Finder's Find <www.apple.com/support>.

BACK UP YOUR HARD DRIVE

A computer backup is nothing more than a duplicate copy of a file. But, copies stored in the same location as the original don't protect against disaster. If your hard drive crashes or your laptop is lost or stolen, you may lose both the original and your backup copy.

A true backup stores copies on two separate devices. The devices you use depend on your needs, time, and budget. A backup plan helps you get organized to make regular backups of all your important files. Check out these options to see what works best for your situation:

HOW OFTEN WILL YOU BACK UP YOUR FILES?

☐ Monthly: Full data backup

☐ Weekly or After Any Major Research Session: All working files, including your Genealogy folder

☐ Daily or Hourly: Working files

WHERE WILL YOU SAVE YOUR BACKUP FILES?

☐ External USB Hard Drive

☐ Home Network Server

☐ Recordable DVDs or CDs

☐ USB Flash Drives

☐ Online Cloud Storage

WHAT FILES WILL BE INCLUDED IN YOUR MONTHLY OR SCHEDULED BACKUPS?

☐ Genealogy Folder

☐ Genealogy Database Files

☐ Pictures

☐ Movies

☐ Family History Projects

HOW WILL YOU BACK UP YOUR FILES?

☐ Automated or manual backup program

☐ Mac users: Mac OS Time Machine

☐ PC users: backup software

Backup Basics

Regular backups don't have to be a hassle. If you find yourself forgetting to schedule backups, or you just want the peace of mind of an automated system, look for a backup program with custom scheduling. See the Resources section at the end of this chapter for automated backup systems and online cloud backup storage options.

EXTERNAL STORAGE OPTIONS. With storage prices continuing to drop, you have several economical choices for secondary storage devices. Remember, however, that any device is subject to damage from disaster or handling, and smaller devices may be easily lost or stolen.

- Online Cloud Storage: free and inexpensive options available, secure, automated, requires network connection
- External USB Hard Drive: portable, inexpensive
- USB Flash Drive: great for travel, quick backups
- SD Media Card: ultra compact, good in a pinch
- CD/DVD: requires burning software
- Network Storage Device: requires network know-how

Add a Tag to Your Flash Drive

Don't leave home without adding a "luggage tag" to your external storage device. Add an ID file: plug the drive in to your computer, open a new text file using your computer Text Editor and type: If found, please return this drive to [your name and phone number]. Thank you.

Save the file with the file name: IF FOUND.

Eject the drive and add a label with your name and phone number to the exterior. With these IDs in place, if you accidentally leave your flash drive in the library microfilm scanner, there is a very good chance it will be returned.

THE MAGIC OF METADATA

If you've ever wished for a way to add more information to your file names like keywords, subject, or location, you will be happy to discover the magic of metadata, a word that simply means data about data. Professional photographers and institutional archivists have a lot in common when it comes to managing image files. Photographers and archivists handle vast quantities of images; it would be impossible to search and find exactly what they need without a careful vocabulary of special words to point them to the files. By adding keywords, or tags, the files become quickly searchable. To make the system even more efficient, archives rely on a controlled vocabulary that has become a standard language used in many universities, museums, and libraries.

Your family archive doesn't need an official language, but you will save time and frustration by establishing a sort of metadata vocabulary to use when tagging images in your own collection. Start by keying information for your family archive images, and then begin adding metadata to your regular office files.

Add Metadata to Your Files

Most files offer easy entry to file metadata through the Get Info (Mac) or File Properties (PC) option under the File Menu. Click on a file to select it, and go to File: Get Info or File Properties. You should see a box with information about the file name, file size, kind of file, date created, date modified, etc. The amount of custom information you can add depends on the kind of file you are viewing. Most often, you can add comments, keywords, or descriptive words. These words help your computer search faster by focusing on the given field.

Genealogists can take advantage of metadata by adding surnames, localities, and keywords. Photo-organizing software, like Adobe Photoshop Elements, XnView, or Adobe Lightroom, offers keywording abilities to add file metadata. Software programs, like Adobe Acrobat or Adobe Bridge, include advanced options with more data fields allowing, source information to be embedded within the file itself.

RESOURCES

GeneaBloggers Backup Resources **<www.geneabloggers.com/resources-backing-data>**

Automated Backup Systems:

Mac OS Time Machine **<support.apple.com/kb/HT1427>**
Mac Carbon Copy Cloner **<www.bombich.com>**
PC GFI Backup **<www.gfi.com/backup-software-for-business>**

Online Cloud Backup Storage

Apple iCloud **<www.apple.com/icloud>**
Backblaze **<www.backblaze.com>**
Carbonite **<www.carbonite.com>**
Dropbox **<www.dropbox.com>**
Mozy **<www.mozy.com>**

Metadata and Keyword Tagging

Adobe Acrobat, Bridge, Lightroom, Photoshop Elements **<www.adobe.com>**
Apple iPhoto **<www.apple.com>**
XnConvert Photo Software **<www.xnconvert.com>** or **<www.xnview.com>**

PART 3

Root Your Research in Strategies for Success

If you're like me, there's never enough research time for everything on your genealogy to-do list. The list grows longer, but research time seems to grow shorter. To make things worse, every genealogist recognizes that déjà vu moment when we're deep in a microfilm or published index and we think, "Hey, I've already looked at this record."

Effective researchers know that organization is the key to productivity.

Organize the Three Rs—Research, Results, and Records—to work smarter, not longer, so you can check off more items on your genealogy to-do list.

If your habit is to surf the Internet for your ancestors, print out your findings, and then set aside the paper to file "later," decide right now to start replacing those old habits with new, simple habits that will make you a more effective family historian.

HOW TO GET STARTED

You probably know where you need a little help to become a more productive genealogist, whether it's developing a research plan, organizing paperwork, or cleaning up your computer. Jump right to the chapter that addresses your current roadblock and find ideas to help you become a more effective researcher today.

CHAPTER 13 ORGANIZE YOUR RESEARCH: Productive research begins with organized research methods. This chapter outlines effective research strategies with step-by-step ideas, case study examples, and helpful resource checklists.

CHAPTER 14 ORGANIZE YOUR SOURCE CITATIONS: Without proof, there is no truth. This chapter offers an overview of effective citation styles and helpful checklists for working with your archival materials.

CHAPTER 15 ORGANIZE YOUR SOFTWARE SOLUTIONS: Technology can advance your geneal-ogy research by saving time and effort. This chapter will help you discover useful services to fit your needs, both web-based and on your computer

CHAPTER 16 ORGANIZE AND DISCOVER RESEARCH CONNECTIONS ONLINE: Social media ser-vices, blogs, forums, and LIST-SERVs can help you find family and break down brick walls. Use the tips in this chapter to expand your genealogy research.

13

Organize Your Research

Your research plan is a lot like a genealogy GPS device—set your destination and then select your route. Following a plan is a lot faster than stumbling around unfamiliar territory seeing the same landmarks over and over. Determine what you want to discover and then select the best tools to help you reach your goal. Keep good records of where you've searched—the genealogical equal to storing an address in your GPS device—to avoid revisiting the same sources time after time.

Your research plan can be as simple or as detailed as necessary, but it doesn't need to be complicated or time-consuming. The best research plans will save you time and steer you toward your goal with a minimum of distraction and fewer stops along the way.

Unfortunately, the term "research plan" can be a bit confusing. Just what is a research plan? Is it an overall strategy, a printed form used to state goals and objectives, a table of repositories to be consulted, a list of source groups and sources to be searched, or a log of research results?

In genealogy research, the term is used to mean both an overall strategy and a written course of action, although these are two very different tasks. No wonder it's confusing.

This chapter will help you develop an effective research strategy with step-by-step guidelines and case study examples. Popular planning methods will also be introduced with helpful resource checklists to jump-start your research. Resources will direct you to forms, charts, and planning aids.

STRATEGY FOR SUCCESSFUL RESEARCH

Does this sound familiar? You sit down at your computer, or walk into a library, and decide to spend "a few minutes" searching (once again) for your most elusive ancestor. An hour later, you realize that you are revisiting sources you consulted in your last session. You're not making any progress, again. Effective genealogists know that research success begins even before the first Internet query box is completed or the first reel of microfilm is loaded.

> **A Genealogy Research Plan is**
>
> • an overall research strategy and/or
> • a written course of action for conducting a specific search

You have a research goal—to find your ancestor.

What you don't have is a research strategy—a written, step-by-step proposal to achieve your goal.

An effective research strategy includes at least four major steps

1. Set a goal.
   a. Identify the problem, or goal.
   b. Break down the goal into smaller, focused mini-goals.
2. Decide what sources to search.
   a. List record groups that may provide a solution.
   b. List specific sources to search.
   c. Locate repositories holding the sources you need.
3. Search the source.
   a. Note the results of your search, positive or negative.
   b. Copy the raw information.
   c. Record the source citation data.
4. Analyze the information.
   a. Evaluate the information.
   b. Record your findings in your notes and database program.
   c. Determine your next step.
5. Repeat from step 1.

As you become more experienced with the research process, you may find these steps becoming almost automatic. One round of setting goals, determining likely sources, searching, analyzing, and recording information will lead smoothly to a second and third round of information gathering, analysis, and input. It is a cyclical process but should always be moving you forward. Let's look at each step a bit further.

STEP 1: SET A GOAL

Remember that family archive you inherited from a loved one? Like any large project, the dozens of boxes, bags, and bins may have seemed overwhelming at first. Use the same tools that helped you organize your archive to help you gain control of your research. Begin with some hard thinking to set realistic goals. Your **research goal** is the big prize; **mini-goals** are milestones along the way that help you achieve your goal.

STATE YOUR OVERALL RESEARCH GOAL. Identifying an ancestor's parents, learning a marriage date, or unravelling a relationship are each *big* goals that become more do-able when viewed as the end result of a series of smaller tasks. Write down your overall research goal in a clear, direct statement. Include names, dates, and localities.

IDENTIFY YOUR MINI-GOALS. Consider your time, energy, and other commitments to set realistic mini-goals that will help move you toward your destination. In the same way that you organize an archive box by box, think about your research goals as many steps toward an overall objective. Be realistic in determining how much (or how little) time you have available to spend in local repositories or surfing the Internet for answers. Always begin your search at home, then widen the scope to include other family members, local and online resources, and then resources more difficult to use.

What's your destination, or your goal? What do you want to learn?

You may want to discover the identity of your paternal grandmother, but there may be several stops or even traffic detours before you arrive at your destination. Think of those stops as opportunities to collect more fuel for your journey—just as you have to refuel your car on a long trip. Any piece of information you verify or disprove will help you move closer to your final goal and keep you on course.

CASE STUDY
My Search for Sam Chamblin

For years I have been trying to confirm or deny my grandmother's story that her grandfather, Samuel Chamblin, was the son of Samuel and Caroline Chamblin of Springfield, Illinois. The 1850 census records show a son of a likely age, but his name is Charles. Are Samuel and Charles the same person?

My Goal: Determine the identity of Arline Allen Kinsel's grandfather. Arline noted that her grandfather, Samuel Chamblin, died in 1889, in Kansas City, Missouri, at the age of forty-three. He was thought to be the son of Samuel and Caroline Chamblin of Springfield, Illinois.

Mini-Goal #1: Confirm death information for Samuel Chamblin [Jr].

Mini-Goal #2: Find birth information for Charles / Samuel [Jr] Chamblin.

Each mini-goal moves me closer to my ultimate goal, and with limited (and sporadic) research hours available for my search, completing a smaller mini-goal is a real boost in my overall sense of achievement. It may take several of these mini-goals to reach my final objective, but I feel like I am making progress when I complete each smaller mini-goal.

Start with the *big* goal, and then break it down into logical mini-goals. Each of these mini-goals can be the focus of one research plan.

STEP 2: DECIDE WHAT SOURCES TO SEARCH

Spend some time thinking about the ancestor you are seeking in the context of his or her own time. Review local and state history for clues to activities or events that may have involved your ancestor. Children's history books and textbooks provide a good overview for reference; check out your child's school books for hints you can use in your search. This will give an idea of sources you should search.

Sources hold the information we seek, but the information can often be found in more than one source. For example, where should I look for the birth information I hope to find? I could start listing individual sources for likely birth information, but it's more useful to do a little brainstorming and come up with a list of record groups, or source types, that may hold the information I need.

Use Checklists

Use record group checklists to help focus your search efforts. It will be most helpful to add those source groups that apply specifically to your ancestor. If you are looking for birth information, and know that your ancestor was orphaned or adopted, you will want to include Adoption Records and Delayed or Amended Birth Records in your initial list of potential sources. Use the comprehensive Records Checklist at the end of this chapter to further identify potential record groups and sources for your search.

Don't overlook military records for both male and female ancestors. Men were often required to register for service, although they may not have actually served in the armed forces. Women may have applied for pension, disability, or other benefits related to service by a husband, son, father, or brother.

Reference a timeline of military history for the United States to determine your ancestor's possible involvement in wars or battles. One good online source is the United States Military Timeline available at **<www.wvc.edu/library/research/gen/RBGenMil_timeline.html>**. Refer to local history for references to skirmishes and lesser-known engagements. The Military Information Checklist at the end of this chapter provides an overview of United States military record groups that may include your ancestor. Check the Resources section in this chapter for links to helpful military timelines.

After determining the broad record groups that may hold the key to your puzzle, list potential sources and repositories likely to hold those records. Start with the most obvious and most available. Remember, copies of many of the records you need may have been given to your ancestor. Always begin your record search at home.

Sources for Sam Chamblin's Vital Records

As I identify sources to help me confirm the birth of Samuel Chamblin, I should include Civil War pension and service records because he most likely lived in the mid- to late–nineteenth century. In addition, I should search for him by name in United States Population Census Records beginning in 1850.

I could decide to travel to Springfield, Illinois, to look firsthand for clues to Samuel's birth; but that wouldn't be a very good use of my time, or funds. A better choice is to start close to home and then widen the search. My research strategy is growing to include not only what I want to learn, but where I will look for the answers;

Mini-Goal #1—Confirm death information for Samuel Chamblin [Jr].

1. Reexamine notes left behind by my grandmother for clues.
2. Search online databases and sources for vital records, census, military, and newspaper records.
3. Order relevant microfilms for viewing.
4. Write local resources for information.

Mini-Goal #2—Find birth information for Charles / Samuel [Jr] Chamblin.

1. Search online databases and sources for vital records, census, military, and newspaper records.
2. Order relevant microfilms for viewing.
3. Write local resources for information.

STEP 3: SEARCH THE SOURCE

Search each listed source and examine information for clues. It's not enough to just jot down the information you need, such as the birthdate or birthplace. For every "hit," you will certainly find negative results as well.

Use the following Source Searched worksheet for each source you search, whether or not you find what you are looking for.

Time spent recording negative as well as positive searches is a good investment to maximizing future research time. It will be easy to see the results of previous searches to avoid revisiting the same sources.

Copying information doesn't necessarily mean you have to create painstaking handwritten notes; you may prefer to type up notes on your computer word processor, photocopy relevant pages, save online search results to your hard drive, or to snap a digital picture of the source.

SOURCE SEARCHED

Title of publication or database _____

    Author _____

    Page number, website URL _____

    Publisher, place and date of publication _____

    Date of your search _____

    Date Web page accessed _____

Name and variations used for the search _____

Results: positive or negative _____

Raw Information

    Transcribed _____

    Photocopied or scanned _____

    Saved as digital image _____

This form is available for download at **<familytreeuniversity.com/familykeepsakes>.**

STEP 4: ANALYZE THE INFORMATION

It's not enough to simply copy data from the source directly to your genealogy database program. Good researchers spend time evaluating new information and asking key questions including:

- Is it true?
- Is the source reliable?
- Do other sources agree with this information?

Record your analysis in your notes. The notation could be as simple as: *This birthdate agrees with the date in the Family Bible.*

As you evaluate the information you've found, you'll likely start forming your next search strategy. The strategy may be as obvious as searching the next record group on your list, or it may be an entirely new avenue of research suggested by your findings. Include your ideas in your notes, and develop another round of research incorporating this new information.

Effective research is not a linear process, moving from point A to point B. It is a round-trip effort. With thoughtful planning, an organized researcher will move from point A to point B, and then return to point A again with new information and plans to visit another destination.

How you record your research strategy is less important than actually doing it. In the next section, I outline a few traditional and not-so-traditional methods for recording your research strategy.

PLANNING METHODS

In elementary school we learned that there are a number of ways to learn a new skill. Some people learn best by verbal instructions, others need to see things written down either in words or visual pictures. Still others learn best by actually doing a task themselves. You probably already know how you work best; capitalize on that knowledge and develop a planning method that plays to your best skills.

Characteristics of a Good Planning Method

A workable Research Planning Method needs to:

1. BE FAIRLY EASY TO LEARN AND MASTER. Give yourself three projects to try out a new system. The first run will be a learning experience and may take some time. By the second use, you should feel more comfortable, and may even be adapting the system to your personal style. By the third project, the system should feel like an old friend, easy and adaptable. If it's not working, try something different.

2. INCLUDE CATEGORY LABELS AS PROMPTS FOR RESEARCH ESSENTIALS. Any system is only as good as the information it holds. If a form doesn't prompt you for something you need later, it hasn't done its job. On the other hand, if there are too many category labels for extraneous information, you will waste time filling in squares, ignore the labels, or become confused by the deluge of text. A good system leaves room to expand, yet doesn't clutter the interface with unnecessary detail or empty boxes.

3. SUIT YOUR WORK STYLE. Spreadsheets suit some people, smooth paper and a fountain pen suit others. Think about your annual calendar or planner purchase—chances are you return to the same format year after year. Oh, you may try something new once in a while, but if it doesn't work out, you probably go right back to that three-ring daily planner or desktop software that seems "just right." Your genealogy planning method should be a good fit, too. There is no one-size-fits-all method.

What's best for you? Find a system that works, and stick with it. It's fine to try something new, but if you find yourself thinking, *I was doing fine the old way*, or *I just can't get the hang of this new-fangled system*, clearly, it's time to look again.

Here are a few ways to plan research that you may have not considered. One might be just what you are looking for.

Traditional Research Log

The traditional Research Log is a form recommended by many genealogy instructors and often available at libraries and research centers. This form may also be called a Research Plan, Research Calendar, Source Log, or Source List. It's sometimes used as an all-purpose, all-in-one record for planning, for listing sources, and for recording source results. See the Resources section for links to research forms you can download.

Traditionally, research logs were printed forms filled out by hand. As technology advances, many people are moving away from paper records. Many researchers have set up an electronic Research Log using a word-processing document. The Log can be modified and stored on their computer, shared via e-mail, and transferred using a flash drive. This electronic version works well for many researchers, especially veteran genealogists who work almost automatically within the familiar interface.

Whether you use a paper or electronic Research Log form, the objective is the same. These forms attempt to save time by combining the Research Strategy and Research Log in one chart or document. Typically, the form may include:

- research goal
- ancestor's name, birth, and death dates
- ancestor's locality
- repository to be searched, hours, address
- search date
- call numbers
- source title, author, date, page number, website, keywords
- reason for search
- search results (positive or negative)

- reference to notes page
- reference to photocopy or digital image

That's a lot of information to include in one form. I've found that paper forms, and their word-processor counterparts, never seem to have exactly the right categories for my project or the space provided is either too large or too small for my needs. In addition, I tend to misplace loose sheets of paper, and I don't like carrying a heavy briefcase or notebook. The traditional Research Log form may be efficient for tracking ongoing research for a specific problem, but because it's not suitable for all research goals, it was easy to set the list aside, leaving an incomplete record of sources searched.

I found more success planning and tracking my research with different documents for different tasks: a Research Plan, Source and Repository Checklists, and Research Logs to record search results.

Moving to a computer system would seem like a no-brainer for someone like me, but I have yet to devise the perfect research plan form. My best efforts are more a work-in-progress, but what's wrong with that? My research changes from project to project, why shouldn't my research planning be adaptable too? The best research plan is the one that works for you.

Lately, I find that I am using three different approaches to develop my overall Research Plan, depending on the size and scope of my goal. Each approach incorporates a few standard blocks of information, and goes on to expand as needed. I've found that my no-one-size-fits-all approach suits my diverse research needs and my rather eclectic research style.

Sketch or Mind Map a Research Plan

Are you a visual thinker? A doodler? If so, you may find it helpful to draw a mind map of your research plan. Mind mapping is a proven technique for project planning and problem solving. It can also be especially useful for ordering timelines, visualizing family relationships, and brainstorming research ideas.

Roll out a large sheet of white shelf paper. Write your goal in the center and draw a bubble or cloud around it. Then start writing down everything

Mind-Mapping Applications

iMindMap, PC, Mac, Mobile
<www.thinkbuzan.com>
iThoughts, Mobile <www.ithoughts.co.uk>
MindMeister, Web and Mobile <www.mindmeister.com>
NovaMind, PC, Mac <www.novamind.com>
XMind, PC, Mac, Linux <www.xmind.net>

Learn Mind Mapping

Mind-Mapping Strategies
<www.mindmappingstrategies.com>
Biggerplate <www.biggerplate.com>

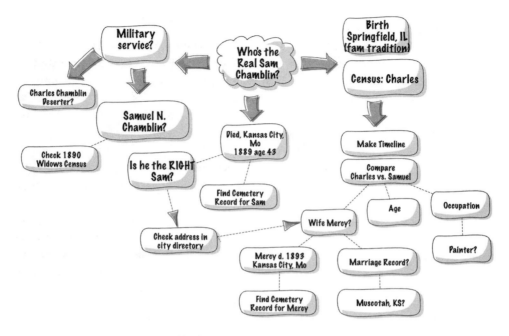

Mind Map research brainstorming

you can think of that is related to that goal. Draw connectors to show the relationships between the words. You may write down a word and then think of two or three other words specifically related. Write those down and connect them all. Your research mind map may begin to look like a great big family tree. New ideas will sprout more twigs and branches. Let your inner artist play a bit; you may find creative research angles you'd never considered before.

If you prefer to play with technology more than colored markers, try downloading computer software or mobile device apps that let you brainstorm on screen. Mobile versions also offer portability; you may not want to tote your poster-sized mind map on a research trip.

Mind mapping is a good start for brainstorming and overall planning, but don't stop there! Take one branch from your mind map and use it as a mini-goal. Work out your research strategies and transfer specifics to an expanded mind map or to a more traditional format where you can also record the results of your search.

The best part about mind mapping is that it's fun! One idea leads to another and another until soon you may have an entire research plan mapped out and ready to go.

Write a Research Plan

If you are the kind of person who usually reads the directions *before* trying something new, you may recognize yourself as visual/verbal learner. You might find mind mapping useful, but you probably fill your maps with a lot of words, too. Go ahead, take your written notes a step further and turn them into a step-by-step plan to reach your goal.

Fans of paper and pen often have a favorite notebook or paper size. Don't feel constrained to use only letter-sized sheets. At this early stage, focus on your proposed research rather than future filing. You can scan your notes and save them as letter-sized sheets for printing as necessary.

I prefer notebooks that are small enough to easily fit in my purse or tote bag but still have enough room for extended lists and goals. My notebook has sections for different surnames and localities, as well as a section for random thoughts and possibilities. I number and date each page for easy cross-referencing.

Sometimes I work up a complex research plan in my computer word-processing program and print out a copy that I fold and tuck inside my notebook. I don't really worry about making these research plans uniform in size and shape for ease in filing; I hope to reach my research goal, transfer my findings, and move on to the next problem. Any notes that need to be filed can be removed from a notebook or photocopied or scanned to standard-sized paper.

Use a Checklist Research Plan

Almost everyone loves checklists and the satisfaction of ticking off a completed task. Some research goals are fairly straightforward and suitable for a to-do-style list. If you like working with lists and clear, concise direction, you may find yourself developing research to-do lists as part of your overall plan.

Checklists are easy to maintain in a variety of formats—on the computer, mobile phone or device, in a notebook, or as part of a daily calendar/planner. Decide on the format that works best for you and stick with it. You don't want to waste time searching for your list when you could be searching for your ancestors.

RESOURCES

Develop a Genealogy Research Plan

"The Research Cycle," by Karen Clifford, AG **<www.genealogy.com/84_clifford.html>**
National Genealogy Society **<www.ngsgenealogy.org>**
Federation of Genealogical Societies **<www.fgs.org>**
Also consult your local genealogy society and national genealogy associations for information on developing a research plan.

U.S. Military History

United States Military Timeline
<www.wvc.edu/library/research/gen/RBGenMil_timeline.html>

Americans at War, Online Exhibit from the Smithsonian Institute
<americanhistory.si.edu/militaryhistory/exhibition/flash.html>

Forms and Charts

Ancestry.com **<www.ancestry.com/trees/charts/researchcal.aspx>**

Family Tree Magazine **<familytreemagazine.com/freeforms>**

FamilySearch Research Log (from the FamilySearch Research Wiki)
<www.familysearch.org/learn/wiki>

Birth Information Checklist

FIRST, SEARCH FOR:

Birth Certificates, Registration
- ☐ at home
- ☐ city, county, state record offices

Baby Books, Announcements, Mementos
- ☐ at home

Family Bible, Photos, Heirlooms
- ☐ at home
- ☐ other family members
- ☐ online family trees, websites

Baptism, Confirmation,
Other Religious Records
- ☐ at home
- ☐ church

U.S. Census Information
- ☐ agriculture schedules
- ☐ Civil War veterans schedules
- ☐ defective, dependent, and delinquent schedules
- ☐ federal population schedules for years _____
- ☐ manufacturing/industry schedules
- ☐ mortality schedules
- ☐ American Indian special censuses
- ☐ school censuses
- ☐ slave schedules
- ☐ social statistics schedules
- ☐ state and local censuses

Birth Announcements
- ☐ newspapers

THEN, SEARCH FOR:

Death Certificates
- ☐ at home
- ☐ city, county, state record offices

Funeral Program, Guest Book, Memorial Card
- ☐ at home

Funeral Record
- ☐ funeral home
- ☐ church and minister's records

Cemetery Records, Gravestone Inscriptions
- ☐ cemeteries
- ☐ gravestones

Will, Probate, Guardianship, Custody Records
- ☐ city, county, state record offices

Obituaries
- ☐ newspapers
- ☐ professional journals
- ☐ club and organization newsletters

Land and Property Records
- ☐ city, county, federal records

School records, yearbooks
- ☐ school libraries

Military Records
- ☐ local newspapers
- ☐ military records

Employment
- ☐ professional licenses and organizations
- ☐ railroad, mining, factory, business records
- ☐ insurance records

Foreign Births
- ☐ immigration, naturalization, citizenship records

FOR ADOPTIONS ADD:

Delayed and Amended Birth Registrations
- ☐ city, county, federal records

Adoption Records
- ☐ court records

This list is available to download online at **<familytreeuniversity.com/ familykeepsakes>**.

Death Information Checklist

FIRST, SEARCH FOR:

Death Certificates
- ☐ at home
- ☐ city, county, state record offices

Funeral or Memorial Program, Guest Book, Memorial Card
- ☐ at home

Family Bible, Photos, Heirlooms
- ☐ at home
- ☐ other family members
- ☐ online family trees, websites

U.S. Census Information
- ☐ agriculture schedules
- ☐ Civil War veterans schedules
- ☐ defective, dependent, and delinquent schedules
- ☐ federal population schedules for years

    _____

- ☐ manufacturing/industry schedules
- ☐ mortality schedules
- ☐ American Indian special censuses
- ☐ school censuses
- ☐ slave schedules
- ☐ social statistics schedules
- ☐ state and local censuses

Cemetery Records, Gravestone Inscriptions
- ☐ cemeteries
- ☐ gravestones

Obituaries
- ☐ newspapers
- ☐ professional journals
- ☐ club and organization newsletters

Retirement and Pension Records
- ☐ Social Security Death Index
- ☐ Railroad Retirement Board
- ☐ other retirement records

THEN, SEARCH FOR:

Will, Probate, Guardianship, Custody Records
- ☐ city, county, state record offices

Funeral Record
- ☐ funeral home
- ☐ church and minister's records

Land and Property Records
- ☐ city, county, federal records

Court Records
- ☐ city, county, federal records

Military Records
- ☐ local newspapers
- ☐ military records (see Military Checklist)

Employment
- ☐ professional licenses and organizations
- ☐ railroad, mining, factory, business records
- ☐ insurance records

This list is available to download online at <**familytreeuniversity.com/familykeepsakes**>.

Marriage Information Checklist

FIRST, SEARCH FOR:

Marriage Certificates, Bonds, Licenses
- ☐ at home
- ☐ city, county, state record offices

Marriage Banns, Records
- ☐ church and minister's records

Wedding Albums
- ☐ at home

Family Bible, Photos, Heirlooms
- ☐ at home
- ☐ other family members
- ☐ online family trees, websites

Engagement and Marriage Announcements
- ☐ newspapers

U.S. Census Information
- ☐ agriculture schedules
- ☐ Civil War veterans schedules
- ☐ defective, dependent, and delinquent schedules
- ☐ federal population schedules for years _____
- ☐ manufacturing/industry schedules
- ☐ mortality schedules
- ☐ American Indian special censuses
- ☐ school censuses
- ☐ slave schedules
- ☐ social statistics schedules
- ☐ state and local censuses

Cemetery Records, Gravestone Inscriptions
- ☐ cemeteries
- ☐ gravestones

Obituaries
- ☐ newspapers
- ☐ professional journals
- ☐ club and organization newsletters

THEN, SEARCH FOR:

Will, Probate, Guardianship, Custody Records
- ☐ city, county, state record offices

Land and Property Records
- ☐ city, county, federal records

Court Records
- ☐ city, county, federal records

Military Records
- ☐ local newspapers
- ☐ military records (see Military Checklist)

This list is available to download online at **<familytreeuniversity.com/familykeepsakes>**.

Divorce Information Checklist

FIRST, SEARCH FOR:

Divorce Petition and Decree
- ☐ at home (copies)
- ☐ divorce court records

Divorce Notices
- ☐ newspapers

THEN, SEARCH FOR:

U.S. Census Information
- ☐ agriculture schedules
- ☐ Civil War veterans schedules
- ☐ defective, dependent, and delinquent schedules
- ☐ federal population schedules
- ☐ manufacturing/industry schedules
- ☐ mortality schedules
- ☐ American Indian special censuses
- ☐ school censuses
- ☐ slave schedules
- ☐ social statistics schedules
- ☐ state and local censuses

Will, Probate, Guardianship, Custody Records
- ☐ city, county, state record offices

Land and Property Records
- ☐ city, county, federal records

Court Records
- ☐ city, county, federal records

This list is available to download online at **<familytreeuniversity.com/familykeepsakes>**.

Residence Information Checklist

FIRST, SEARCH FOR:

U.S. Census Information
- ☐ agriculture schedules
- ☐ Civil War veterans schedules
- ☐ defective, dependent, and delinquent schedules
- ☐ federal population schedules for years
  _____
- ☐ manufacturing/industry schedules
- ☐ mortality schedules
- ☐ American Indian special censuses
- ☐ school censuses
- ☐ slave schedules
- ☐ social statistics schedules
- ☐ state and local censuses

THEN, SEARCH FOR:

Locality and Address
- ☐ city directories
- ☐ telephone books
- ☐ town and county maps
- ☐ voters' registration
- ☐ tax records
- ☐ newspapers
- ☐ unclaimed mail notices

Membership Lists
- ☐ church records
- ☐ clubs and organizations
- ☐ employment rosters

Land and Property Records
- ☐ city, county, federal records

Town Records
- ☐ road crew roster
- ☐ tax rolls
- ☐ voting records

Published Genealogy Checklist

Your ancestor or family may be included in a published or privately prepared genealogy or family history. Information in these resources is not always accurate, but can provide clues for further research and help corroborate your research.

FIRST, SEARCH FOR:

Genealogy and Pedigree Charts
- ☐ at home
- ☐ family members
- ☐ lineage society databases
- ☐ International Genealogy Index

Samplers, Hand-Drawn Family Trees
- ☐ at home
- ☐ family members

THEN, SEARCH FOR:

Family Histories, Biographies
- ☐ indexes, catalogs
- ☐ genealogical society journals
- ☐ oral history projects
- ☐ manuscript collections
- ☐ record transcriptions

County and Local History
- ☐ published county and local histories
- ☐ county maps
- ☐ historical society publications
- ☐ city directories
- ☐ WPA publications
- ☐ oral history projects
- ☐ church and organization histories

This list is available to download online at **<familytreeuniversity.com/familykeepsakes>**.

Military Information Checklist

Identify conflicts your ancestor may have served in by consulting a historical timeline, such as the online United States Military Timeline **<www.wvc.edu/library/research/gen/RBGenMil_timeline.html>**. Then, look for records in the following record groups.

FIRST, SEARCH FOR:

Military Papers, Enlistment, Notices, etc.
- ☐ at home (copies)

Correspondence
- ☐ at home

Photographs
- ☐ at home
- ☐ local newspaper

Memorabilia, Military Service Awards
- ☐ at home
- ☐ diaries, journals
- ☐ at home

Cemetery Records
- ☐ local cemeteries

Obituaries, Funeral Records
- ☐ at home
- ☐ local newspapers

THEN, SEARCH FOR:

Military Affiliations
- ☐ veteran organizations

Military Records: Registration, Draft, Enlistment, Service
- ☐ online databases
- ☐ military service record repositories

Service Branch and Unit Records
- ☐ online websites
- ☐ veteran associations
- ☐ museums and libraries

14

Organize Your Source Citations

My grandmother Arline and her sister Mercy were enthusiastic amateur genealogists. As a teenager, Great Aunt Mercy prepared a printed descendent list for her family, and years later she lovingly crafted a beautiful family history book for her great-niece. The parchment paper pages are still crisp with gilt and brightly colored paint; the hand-drawn pedigree charts are rich with names, dates, and places. Only one thing is missing to make this treasure even more valuable—sources.

As my charming mom quite emphatically said, "What do you mean 'sources'? I know it!"

How did Great Aunt Mercy really know that Samuel Chamblin was a cousin to Jefferson Davis? How did she make the connection to Roger Williams of Rhode Island? Why did she think Amy Brown was a descendent of Chad Brown, founder of Brown University?

A few footnotes quote relatives or list reference books, but most of Mercy's family genealogy is presented as a beautiful but unsubstantiated theory. I have spent years checking family lines, establishing a chain of sources, and working to confirm or deny Mercy's work.

What I do know is that my grandmother, Arline, was a more careful researcher than Mercy. Numerous letters in Arline's papers bear witness to her ongoing genealogy correspondence with historical societies, researchers, and repositories. Letters written by Mercy to her sister Arline show an ongoing discussion between the two sisters as they tried to document their family tree. One sister wanted written proof; the other wanted family stories.

One thread that runs through their letters is as fresh today as it was nearly one hundred years ago: *without proof, there is no truth.*

As much as I am grateful for the head start with their genealogy work, if Mercy and Arline had made better source notes, I wouldn't be repeating old research today.

This chapter explains citation basics and offers practical ideas for documentation. Resources include handy checklists for catching citation specifics and links to further information.

WHAT'S THE SOURCE OF YOUR SOURCE?

Remember when research meant hardbound books shelved in brick libraries? Those were the days! Assembling a bibliography for a research paper was a simple affair: author, title, publication information.

When did things get so complicated? Photocopy machines, scanners, digital cameras, and the Internet have made it easy to produce and distribute multiple copies of originals. We no longer have to travel to a brick-and-mortar archive to laboriously view microfilmed census images. Those same images are now digitized, indexed, and available online as duplicate originals waiting to be viewed from our own home. Wonderful, you might say; that is, until you need to create a source citation.

If the online image is consulted, it is no longer sufficient to cite the book itself as the source of information. The reason for this is obvious if you have ever been confronted with an online census image where the lines of the page you need are obscured by a folded page or blurred beyond recognition. An original source and each copy may contain all kinds of variations, including:

- blurring due to poor digitizing
- wayward items, such as paper clips, bookmarks, and thumbs on the original copy obscuring portions of the text
- inaccurate index references or tagging
- missing and out-of-order pages
- annotations and corrections
- misplaced sections

If you had a hard time locating a document the first time and finally found it by searching a second or third database, imagine the difficulty someone may have retracing your steps without a careful citation. Future researchers need directions to the exact source used, not the damaged images along the way.

ORIGINAL AND DERIVATIVE SOURCES

As you examine a source for information, it's important to be aware of the type of document you are reading. Is it an original or a derivative?

ORIGINAL SOURCES are in their first form. Period. An original source is something that exists as it was created. Technically, even microfilmed census records are not originals; that status has to be reserved for the paper–and-ink copies made by the census taker. However, as citation expert Elizabeth Shown Mills notes in her book *Evidence Explained: Citing History Sources from Artifacts to Cyberspace*, often "image copies of an original record when produced by an authoritative or reliable agency—as with microfilm or digital copies produced to preserve the originals or to provide wider access to them" are considered as original sources (page 826).

DERIVATIVE SOURCES are materials produced by copying, extracting, or otherwise manipulating the original. A community index of census records is a derivative source.

To go back to the example of the letter my grandmother wrote to her mother, each of the following is a derivative of the original source letter:

- a transcription
- an extract
- an index of names and places used in the letter
- a photocopy of the letter
- a photograph of the letter

SOURCES VS. CITATIONS

Genealogists talk a lot about sources and how to cite them. Some researchers are sticklers for formal academic-style references. Some start out with good citation practices but become frustrated by complicated style guides, and eventually become less conscientious. Others follow a haphazard citation style of partial source information, cut and paste from internet sites, and photocopied title pages from books. Still others don't see a need for citing sources at all. (If I had to assign myself to one of these categories, I'd admit that I don't mind citing sources.)

So which came first, the source or the citation?

SOURCE (noun)—a person, place, or thing from which something originates; *She was the source of his happiness.* In genealogy research: The *1850 U.S. Population Schedule Census* is the source used for establishing the name of my great-grandfather.

SOURCE (verb)—to obtain from a particular person, place or thing; *The exotic spice was sourced from the Middle East.* In genealogy research: *Be careful to source your information.*

A genealogical source could be almost anything all, from a printed document to a telephone interview or an e-mail. Sometimes, information from several sources is analyzed to determine a relationship or establish a fact.

While a *source* provides information, a *citation* describes exactly how to locate the source.

CITATION (noun)—a reference to the origin of the information pointing directly to the exact materials consulted. *The citation directed him to the U.S. Federal Census of 1850 for the Edward Thompson household in Woodstock, Windsor County, Vermont.*

Genealogy citations can be constructed using different formats depending on their intended use. Society journals use their own house style while historical societies and newsletters may require a different style.

WHY BOTHER WITH CITATIONS?

That's fine for writers, you might think, *but I don't intend to publish my research. It's for my own use. Why should I bother with citations?* There are three reasons every genealogist should cite their sources.

1. TO GUIDE OTHERS IN YOUR RESEARCH FOOTSTEPS. Good research is repeatable; your descendants and fellow researchers should be able to follow your research trail and locate your sources.

2. TO TEST OR REEXAMINE EVIDENCE. A genealogist is never truly "finished" researching a family line. New evidence—and newfound relatives—may appear at any time, prompting old hypotheses to be reevaluated, or a fresh look at your conclusions may show an illogical date that needs double checking.

3. TO PREPARE INFORMATION FOR PUBLICATION. Time changes all of us. One day you might like to publish a short ancestor sketch of one your more colorful relatives, but you're held back by the difficulty in retracing your steps to find and write the citations required by your local genealogy society bulletin.

Always take time to document your sources, one never knows what the future will hold.

FEARLESS CITATIONS MADE EASY

Source notes do not have to be cryptic and confusing. Let it be your goal to craft citations that are

- **CLEAR:** easy to understand
- **CONCISE:** contain all information necessary and no more
- **DIRECT:** point future researchers to the source

WHAT'S THE BEST CITATION METHOD?

The best citation style is one that is the standard for your project. There's no need to reinvent the proverbial wheel. Citing sources doesn't have to be hard.

As a high school English teacher, I read hundreds of research papers and source lists each year and was continually amazed at the endless variety of citation formats my students submitted.

The requirements were clear and direct: use MLA (Modern Language Association) style citations. Students, however, seemed determined to create their own unique format based on some other style. I often suspected that some were influenced by their parents' high school experience, especially when the daughters of physicists and physicians turned in work with perfect scientific-styled citations.

Genealogy research doesn't demand *perfect* citations; after all, a citation is merely the road map to your source. Strive to give your readers and descendants clear directions so they can follow your footsteps if need be. It's not so much about the comma as it is the turn in the road.

Not All Citations Are Created Equal

You may remember crafting source lists in high school or college. Depending on the subject, you probably followed MLA format for English and humanities papers, *The Chicago Manual of Style* for history papers, or APA (American Psychological Association) form for papers in the social sciences. No doubt, you learned that creating a correct citation was as much an art as a science.

As the Internet has expanded, so have the varied source styles necessary to document information found in e-books, ever-changing websites, e-mail, online journals and databases, and other online resources. It's no longer a simple matter to string together author, title, publisher, date, and place of publication.

Genealogists have always faced a challenge in citing sources due to the vast and diverse nature of research materials. While scientists might chiefly cite work from published journals, genealogists refer to everything from an heirloom, engraved pocket watch to a cemetery transcription to an online census image to an original probate record.

A Citation Style Just for Genealogists

In the same way that scientists can rely on APA style to guide their needs for a scientific citation format, genealogists can rely on a style tailor-made for family history research. *Evidence Explained: Citing History Sources from Artifacts to Cyberspace* by Elizabeth Shown Mills is a citation style guide developed specifically for genealogists. The 880-plus page volume is a resource for citation style filled with extensive samples and discussion that builds on Mills's earlier, and shorter book, *Evidence! Citation & Analysis for the Family Historian.*

EE (as fans call it) may be the gold standard for many genealogists, but it's not required that you use *EE* style in order to provide a source citation. (*EE* is based on *The Chicago Manual of Style.*) Major genealogy journals today continue to require authors to submit their Source List in their specific "house style" or in one of the popular academic formats, such as MLA, *Chicago*, or APA. You can provide thorough source information without conforming to *EE* style, but it might be a bit harder to remember all the different components you need.

One of the chief advantages of Mills's system is her insistence on citing the actual source used, whether it be a print book you hold in your hands or an online e-book version of a digitized copy of the very same book. When you correctly cite the version used, you help anyone who follows in your research footsteps to more easily find the source you consulted.

What's important is not whether you choose *EE* style or *Chicago*, but that you take time to include *all* the information needed to locate the source. Like Elizabeth Shown Mills, and thousands of other genealogists, I think it's easier to use the genealogy industry standard than to bend, fold, and staple another system to suit my needs. I like the way *EE* provides a reference to each item needed for a full and complete citation.

You may prefer to use one of the academic citation forms, and that's okay. But do be prepared to face situations where the document consulted doesn't fit the standard citation format. Whatever citation style you decide to use, be consistent. Read on for more citation style ideas.

CITATION STYLES

Major Academic Style Guides

APA STYLE (American Psychological Association)

Guidebook: *Publication Manual of the American Psychological Association*

Used for: social sciences

Format: author-date in-text citation

Citation: source list presented in Reference page at end of paper

CHICAGO STYLE

Guidebook: *The Chicago Manual of Style*

Used for: history and some humanities; academic style used most often for genealogy

Format: either Notes-Bibiliography (footnotes or endnotes) style or author-date (in-text) style

Citation: bibliography page at end of paper

MLA STYLE (Modern Language Association)

Guidebook: *The MLA Handbook for Writers of Research Papers*

Used for: English and some humanities

Format: author-page in-text citation

Citation: Works Cited page at end of paper

TURABIAN STYLE

Guidebook: *A Manual for Writers of Term Papers, Theses, and Dissertations* by Kate Turabian

Format: based on *The Chicago Manual of Style*, streamlined for student writers

Just for Genealogy and History

EVIDENCE EXPLAINED STYLE

Guidebook: *Evidence Explained: Citing History Sources from Artifacts to Cyberspace* by Elizabeth Shown Mills

Used for: genealogy

Format: footnotes-endnotes

Citation: Source List at end of paper

SOURCING SHORTCUTS

If you still aren't convinced that citing sources is time well spent, ask yourself: Isn't it worse to spend hours (or days) locating a source you forgot to cite the first time? And who says that source citation has to be time consuming? Streamline your work with one of these shortcuts instead of dropping the citation routine altogether.

Use Your Genealogy Software Source Features

Your current genealogy software may be ready to lend citation assistance. More and more of the major genealogy database programs have integrated *Evidence Explained* style with their own source features, making it easy to enter the required information. The software does all the work to build the required citation with commas, periods, and italics exactly where they belong. Well, almost exactly where they belong. There are the inevitable variations, but it is a fairly good compromise to the alternative of correctly handcrafting each citation.

The best sourcing software will be relatively painless to use. If it's so difficult that you grit your teeth just to input your source information, it's time to find another option. Look for a program that gives you understandable prompts for necessary information and the ability to generate a complete source list. While there is no rule that states genealogy sources must be listed in either *Chicago* or *Evidence Explained* style, they will be formatted in one style or another; why not choose the industry standard?

Take another look at your genealogy software to see if the latest version offers this feature. If not, consider reviewing other genealogy programs that can take this job off your shoulders.

Source features to look for in genealogy software:

• ease of use
• logical (to you!) form design
• prompts for all necessary information
• output in *Chicago* or *EE* style
• ability to memorize sources and easily apply to multiple items
• space for notes, memos, comments

Hint: Good genealogy software will prompt you for each detail of a correct citation, making it easier to include all the information needed to retrace your steps.

Build a Personal Source List

Genealogists know that some sources reoccur frequently; you will often need to cite a federal census or local birth registration. Use *Evidence Explained* (or the style of your choice) to craft the correct citation, and then use this as a model for future references to the source. Some researchers develop an extensive *EE* styled source list they use over and over by cutting-and-pasting text. This can be a real timesaver if most of your research relies on the same sources.

Save your custom citations in a single word-processing document or spreadsheet, or in a database program, so you can quickly search and find the entry to use again. The key is consistency. Make a conscious decision to follow one style; I suggest using *Evidence Explained*, *Chicago*, or *Turabian*. Whatever style you choose, use it consistently.

Hint: The citation feature of your genealogy software will provide this consistency without any extra work from you.

Use a Cheat Sheet

Genealogy research doesn't always take place online or near a computer. You may prefer to make handwritten notes, especially when working in a library or in the field.

Did you know that there's an easy way to remember everything you need to include in a source citation? Use a source checklist for the basic information. Worry about crafting the citation later, but get the source information *now*. Add a copy of the handy Source Checklists at the end of this chapter to your research notebook or post one above your desk.

Make Your Own Source Marking Tool

Do you frequently photocopy or scan documents, photos, or other materials? Have you received copies of a document without accompanying documentation? Don't let your materials become orphans, that is sources without a home.

Blogger and citation-advocate footnoteMaven recommends creating a slim source tool to help you keep track of where you found the item instead of relying on cryptic codes or notes on the reverse side of an image. Create a word-processing document with a sheet of narrow strips that you can fill in with source information. Place the strip along the margin of each page of your document or photo that you scan or copy. Reduce the image size if necessary to allow for the source tool. Check out the footnoteMaven's blog **<www.footnotemaven.com>** for practical tips on citing sources.

TRY AN ONLINE CITATION GENERATOR

Students are big fans of doing *everything* online, so it's not surprising that online citation generators are popular and getting better all the time. A citation website will prompt you for the source information and turn out a citation formatted in the style of your choice. Three online citation makers are:

- **BIBME <www.bibme.org>** limited formats, does not include correspondence
- **EASYBIB <www.easybib.com>** free version does not include *Chicago* style; MLA is only style offered for free
- **NOODLEBIB EXPRESS <www.noodletools.com/noodlebib>** free version includes *Chicago* style; cut-and-paste individual citations only; many formats to use, including "Unpublished Paper, Manuscript or Primary Source Document"

Unfortunately, the results will only be as good as the information entered, and you will have to do some extra work to get everything required for a full genealogical citation. It can also be difficult to remember the detailed information required for a correct *EE* style citation. Some free online citation generators limit the number of citations you can create for free, or the formats available.

Following are the results of a free online citation maker for standard family archive item, the personal letter, formatted in *Chicago* style vs. *Evidence Explained* style.

Reference Note

NOODLEBIB *CHICAGO* **STYLE NOTE:**

1. Arline Allen Kinsel, "(Larkspur, Colorado) to 'My dear Mama' [Minnie Kinsel]," letter, October 12, 1919, Arline Allen Kinsel Papers, Privately held by Denise Levenick [ADDRESS FOR PRIVATE USE], Pasadena, California, 2008.

EVIDENCE EXPLAINED **STYLE FIRST REFERENCE NOTE**

1. Arline Allen Kinsel (Larkspur, Colorado) to "My dear Mama" [Minnie Kinsel], letter, 12 October 1919; Arline Allen Kinsel Papers, privately held by Denise Levenick [ADDRESS FOR PRIVATE USE,] Pasadena, California, 2008. Letter was inherited from Minnie Kinsel by her daughter, Arline, and passed on to Minnie's great-granddaughter in 2000.

Bibliography/Source List Entry

NOODLEBIB EXPRESS GENERATED BIBLIOGRAPHY ENTRY

Kinsel, Arline Allen. "(Larkspur, Colorado) to 'My dear Mama' [Minnie Kinsel]." Letter. October 12, 1919. Arline Allen Kinsel Papers. Privately held by Denise Levenick [ADDRESS FOR PRIVATE USE], Pasadena, California, 2008. Letter was inherited from Minnie Kinsel by her daughter, Arline, and passed on to Minnie's great-granddaughter in 2000.

EVIDENCE EXPLAINED **STYLE SOURCE LIST ENTRY**

Kinsel, Arline Allen (Larkspur, Colorado) to "My dear Mama" [Minnie Kinsel]. Letter. 12 October 1919. Privately held by Denise Levenick [ADDRESS FOR PRIVATE USE,] Pasadena, California. 2008.

At first glance, it might seem that NoodleBib has done a great job presenting a citation very close to Mills's *Evidence Explained* style. But, look more closely and you will see that the difference is in the details. While nearly all elements of the citation are placed in proper order and much of the punctuation is also correct, several particular elements will need to be adjusted, including:

1. Source List Entry—add hanging indent.
2. Delete period after name "Kinsel, Arline Allen"; should be at end of item title only.
3. Delete quotation marks: "(Larkspur, Colorado) to 'My dear Mama' [Minnie Kinsel]."
4. Change single quotes to double quotes: 'My dear Mama'.
5. Convert date format to genealogy style: October 12, 1919.
6. Delete unnecessary collection name: Arline Allen Kinsel Papers.
7. Move comma inside bracket: [ADDRESS FOR PRIVATE USE],
8. Move descriptive note from bibliography entry to Reference Note.

If you're looking for a shortcut to easier genealogy citations, online citation generators may not be the best answer. Instead, I encourage you take time to learn a few citation basics and then take advantage of the citation features of your genealogy database software. After all, ancestor hunting is a lot more fun than tracking down commas and periods.

ARCHIVES SOURCE CHECKLIST

Are you headed to a brick-and-mortar archive? Take along this handy checklist to help you remember to collect all the information you need for a correctly crafted citation.

☐ author or creator's name (agency, department, person)
☐ title of the work
☐ date of the work
☐ publication place and publisher
☐ collection or series name
☐ box and folder
☐ page number
☐ repository
☐ date item is viewed
☐ type of item
☐ notes on condition, readability, etc.

For correspondence, photographs, artifacts, and newspapers, see the following specific checklists for additional details. All of these checklists are available as PDF downloads at **<familytreeuniversity.com/familykeepsakes>**.

CORRESPONDENCE SOURCE CHECKLIST

AUTHOR/CREATOR

☐ writer's name (author)
☐ place written from (publication place)
☐ date of letter (note if undated)

RECIPIENT

- ☐ recipient's name
- ☐ recipient's location

CURRENT OWNER

- ☐ current owner/repository
- ☐ owner/repository address
- ☐ date viewed
- ☐ collection or series name
- ☐ box and folder

LETTER

- ☐ number of pages in letter
- ☐ whether or not the envelope is present
- ☐ notes on condition or enclosures

PHOTOGRAPH SOURCE CHECKLIST

- ☐ photographer's name
- ☐ type of image (original, digital, photocopy, etc.)
- ☐ date of photograph (if known)
- ☐ current owner
- ☐ owner's address
- ☐ date viewed
- ☐ collection name
- ☐ description
- ☐ provenance (chain of ownership, if known)
- ☐ notes on condition etc.

ARTIFACT SOURCE CHECKLIST

- ☐ type of item (Bible, scrapbook, journal, quilt, etc.)
- ☐ creator/author's name (if known)
- ☐ date created (if known)
- ☐ current owner
- ☐ owner's address
- ☐ date viewed
- ☐ collection name
- ☐ description
- ☐ provenance (chain of ownership, if known)
- ☐ notes on condition, readability, etc.

NEWSPAPER CLIPPING SOURCE CHECKLIST

For loose, undated, unidentified newspaper clippings:

- ☐ subject of newspaper clipping
- ☐ headline
- ☐ type of item (undated, unidentified clipping, etc.)
- ☐ approximate date (if possible)
- ☐ current owner
- ☐ owner's address
- ☐ date viewed
- ☐ collection name
- ☐ description
- ☐ provenance (chain of ownership, if known)
- ☐ notes on condition, readability, etc.

RESOURCES

Online Citation Generators

BibMe **<www.bibme.org>**
EasyBib **<www.easybib.com>**
NoodleBib Express **<www.noodletools.com/noodlebib>**

Style Guides

RECOMMENDED FOR GENEALOGY

Evidence Explained: Citing History Sources from Artifacts to Cyberspace, by Elizabeth Shown Mills. **<www.historicpathways.com>**

OTHER PROFESSIONAL STYLE GUIDES

APA Style, by the American Psychological Association **<www.apastyle.org>**

Chicago Style, from *The Chicago Manual of Style* **<www.chicagomanualofstyle.org>**

MLA Style, by the Modern Language Association **<www.mla.org/style>**

Turabian Style, by Kate Turabian based on Chicago Style **<www.press.uchicago.edu/books/turabian/turabian_citationguide.html>**

Learn More About Citing Genealogy Sources

Citing Sources, from Cyndi's List **<www.cyndislist.com/citing>**

"Cite Your Genealogy Sources," from Kimberly Powell on About.com
<genealogy.about.com/od/citing/a/sources.htm>

Family Tree Magazine Source Citation Cheat Sheet
<www.familytreemagazine.com/info/genealogyessentials>

footnoteMaven, by Linda Palmer **<www.footnotemaven.com>**

"Genealogy Source Citations Quick Reference," from High-Definition Genealogy
 <www.geneabloggers.com/Citations_Quick_Reference.pdf>

15

Organize Your Software Solutions

My first typewriter was a little plastic toy that I received as a Christmas gift from my grandfather when I was nine years old. I used it to type stories, poems, plays, and letters until I graduated to a portable Smith Corona in junior high school. When I went off to college, my trunk held a used IBM Selectric and a supply of correction fluid. Each new typewriter model offered new features and faster speed.

Like many, I was excited to move to a word processor but continued to use my computer as a fancy typewriter with easy correction and spell-checking. One year I was asked to take on a large project at my school, a two-hundred page review document with sections, chapters, and numerous headings. It all seemed unmanageable until I took the time to work through a computer handbook and a series of online tutorials. I'm still using the tricks I learned for that project with my genealogy research notes.

Are you taking notes using the same method you learned in high school or college, or a computer version of the same method? Your computer is more than an expensive typewriter, and computer software can do much more than simply type a letter to Mom.

Challenge yourself to learn and master a software feature or a new software program on your next long weekend or summer vacation. Learn to efficiently use tables or spreadsheets or discover the time-saving magic of templates. One afternoon spent learning a new software feature can make you an even more effective family historian.

This chapter gives an overview of the different kinds of software and Web services that you may find useful in working with your family archive and your genealogy research.

FIND THE RIGHT SOFTWARE FOR YOU

You're probably familiar with office software suites such as Microsoft Office, OpenOffice, or Apple iWork that offer word-processing, spreadsheet, and presentation software bundled in one product. But did you know that similar software solutions are also available online as Web-based products, and that some are absolutely free? Why should you care? Maybe you think:

- I already have software.
- I don't want to learn a new program.
- I paid for my software, and want to get my dollar's worth.
- I like control over my computer programs.
- My Internet connection is slow or unreliable.
- I'm not sure about all this "cloud-stuff."

Although you may be quite happy with your current software, online programs have a lot to offer. At the very least, they can offer a good solution in many situations, such as:

- preparing or accessing information while traveling
- backup solution when your computer is down
- free access to special software you rarely use
- working between systems or changing platforms (such as PC to Mac)

If you access your bank accounts online, or use online e-mail applications like Yahoo! Mail or Gmail, you've already used Web-based software. For many situations, Internet software is better than a program that you buy and install on your own machine because the programs have no tech problems, no upgrades, and no cost.

Here are a few of considerations for stand-alone and Web-based software:

Stand-Alone Software

This software is purchased as a download or on a disc and installed individually on individual machines, or on a home network. Popular stand-alone software office products include Microsoft Office (Word, Excel, PowerPoint), OpenOffice (free open source software), and Apple iWork (Pages, Numbers, Keynote). Genealogy programs include database software, such as Family Tree Maker, Legacy, Reunion, and RootsMagic.

PROS: You own the software license and can use it until it becomes obsolete. You may have owned a license for many years and feel very comfortable using the program. No Internet connection is needed.

CONS: You must purchase and manually install upgrades. Cost can become expensive. You have to handle software bugs and problems yourself or call a technician for help. If your computer crashes, or is lost or stolen, you have to reinstall the software on a new machine and handle downtime. Software is typically not cross-platform; new editions must be purchased when moving from PC to Mac, for example.

Web-Based Software

Web-based software is used over the Internet inside your browser, although many programs can be configured for offline access. New software is announced often; check it out when you hear about something promising.

Online office software can provide mobile solutions that have many of the same features as your current desktop office software.

PROS: Web-based software is upgraded and maintained by the company that produces it so you are always using the newest version. Many programs are free or low cost, comparable to full downloadable software. Cross-platform compatibility makes it easy to move from PC to Mac or computer to computer. Your documents are available anywhere you have an Internet connection; offline access can be configured for many programs.

CONS: You don't own the license, so you could lose access if the software loses support or is sold to another company. An Internet connection is needed to get started and to create new documents although some programs allow offline viewing.

WORD PROCESSOR

Your word processor is more than an electronic typewriter that never needs correction fluid. For many researchers, it's the first program they open on their computers each day and they use it all day long. But new versions of popular word-processing software offer more than easy correction and spell-check. Many programs now include features that were formerly found in separate drawing, photo, spreadsheet, and outlining software.

You could be missing some great timesavers if you haven't upgraded your software to the current version and explored new features. Find tutorials online and take time to explore a user's manual.

A word-processing software program is best for:
- working with large amounts of text
- working with text, tables, charts, or drawings together in the same document
- working with small groups of data
- working with small amounts of text in a table for quick sorting or summing
- viewing, editing, or analyzing text in multiple ways
- printing, tables, charts, or forms that will fit on one page, portrait or landscape

SPREADSHEET

For many years, I thought spreadsheets were just for number-crunchers; I used various work-arounds to avoid opening one of those scary-looking documents filled with rows and columns. Then I found a set of free census extract forms built as spreadsheet templates and I experienced a wonderful "Aha" moment. I might not be a confident spreadsheet *creator*, but I could learn to be a competent spreadsheet *user*.

Spreadsheets have no equal when it comes to handling large amounts of data or performing mathematical computations. I envy genealogists who have a background with these powerful tools, and am grateful to those who share templates and forms with more novice users.

Spreadsheet software is best for:
- working with large amounts of data
- viewing and sorting data in multiple ways
- viewing data as a chart
- performing complex math calculations
- selecting portions of information to study, print, or share

DATABASE

Databases do a great job organizing and storing information. For many years, the most familiar kind of database was the traditional library card catalog system. Each card held carefully typed information about an item in the library system. Other cards cross-referenced information making it (fairly) easy to find specific information. Oh, there was still the walking fingers routine, and return trips to the card catalog file to decipher scribbled call numbers, but it was a system that worked well for decades. Then, along came the computer, and overnight, it seemed we could call up the same information in a few seconds instead of a few minutes. As any researcher knows, speed wins.

If the word *database* brings to mind genealogy software like Family Tree Maker, Legacy, Reunion, and RootsMagic, you would be considering some of the options available for handling only genealogy information. These software programs are specifically designed to handle genealogical information and offer special fields and features for this purpose. There are many different kinds of databases available. Your computer address book is a database; it uses a form to hold information about each of your contacts.

While some databases are very specific in the kind of information they process, other database programs are more general and offer users the ability to design a custom form to hold information. This kind of software is great for discrete projects, such as tracking a book or DVD collection, or organizing recipes. Database software, such as Microsoft Access, FileMaker, and Bento, are popular general database programs.

Database programs are best for:
- working with large amounts of information with many fields
- inputting and viewing data in a form-style interface or column-style
- selecting portions of information to study, print, or share
- creating data sets to interact with other data sets
- organizing information about data (i.e., a collection)

FINDING THE BEST TOOL FOR THE JOB

Your choice to use a table, a spreadsheet, or a database to organize your records depends on personal preference, experience, and the task at hand. I have found that word-people, like writers and educators, may prefer a table or database solution, and math/science-people often prefer to use a spreadsheet. My favorite program for fast custom databases is FileMaker's Bento, an inexpensive Mac-only program.

When I need to organize information, I first think of using a database. My mind's eye visualizes a traditional card catalog, although I'll be using software. I can design a card, or form, or full-size sheet to hold my information and soon be entering data that appears in a familiar format.

One of my genealogy friends who is a math whiz and former accountant chooses a spreadsheet as her favorite informational tool. In a matter of seconds, she has a columnar format set up and is inputting data into each field. It all looks very official to me, and I admit, it's a faster way to enter data.

My friend taught me to look for and use the Spreadsheet View in my database. It gives me the best of both worlds—fast data entry and a more familiar format for individual records.

As a family historian, you wear many hats, from researcher to archivist to writer to filing clerk. You may feel most comfortable using a word processor and open a new document for everything, but have you ever wondered if there was a more effective tool for the job?

For many tasks, either a table, spreadsheet, or database will accomplish the same goal. But, sometimes it's not efficient to use the software you are most comfortable with. Database forms generally take more time to set up than a simple table or spreadsheet; save your database for working with a large quantity of information. Similarly, a word processor table is great for listing and sorting data, but can be cumbersome if tables exceed the size of the paper; a spreadsheet is a better choice for numerous columns.

One other often-overlooked program is the drawing feature included in many word processors. Use this handy tool to build relationship charts, family trees, or a simple map to your archive collections.

Here are a few more ideas on how to turn standard office software into family history work-horses and expand your toolbox in ways you may not have considered:

	Word Processor Table	Spreadsheet	Free Form Database	Draw Program
Family Archive Inventory	For small archive	Any size archive	Medium to large archive	
Map for Family Archive Collection				x
Timeline	Short duration	x	Medium to long duration	x
Probate Inventory	x	x		
Grantor-Grantee Lists	x	x		
Plot Maps	x			x
Comparing Census Data	Small sets of data	x		
Census Extracts	Focused groups	x		
Cemetery Lists	Focused groups	x	x	
Graveyard Plot Map		x		x
Passenger Manifest Extracts		x		
Family Naming Practices	x	x		
Custom Research Forms, Checklists	x	x	x	
Organizing Photo Projects	Small projects	Any size	Medium to large project	
Source Log	x	x	x	
Indexing Projects		x	x	
Relationship Chart	x	x		x

GENEALOGY DATABASE SOFTWARE

Mention genealogy databases and genealogists will either spring to their feet or sit back with a wary look in their eye. Many genealogists look to a genealogy database as the master tool in their computer toolkit; others have never used one and see no need for it at all.

One thing is for sure—a genealogy database will not do your research or solve your brick-wall problems. When it comes time to figure out a tricky family connection, the results will depend more on your sound research and thoughtful analysis than on how many names and dates you have input to your genealogy database.

So, what can a genealogy database do that a general database program like FileMaker or Access can't do? Well, I suppose that you could build a customized genealogy database to suit your needs, but I certainly don't have the skill set, time, or energy. Do you? I'm a great believer in trailblazers—show me the road and take the first step. I'll follow along, learning from your experiences, and be ready to use my newfound skills to strike out on my own if necessary.

Some of the best advice I ever received on choosing genealogy software came from an online class with genealogist Karen Clifford. Students were required to use one or two specific programs and submit all work as GEDCOM files. GEDCOM is an acronym for **GE**nealogical **D**ata **COM**munication, an exchange format that allows different genealogy database programs to share data, providing a method for users to move their research from one program to another. I learned that it didn't really matter what particular software was used, it was more important that your information could be exported and imported elsewhere.

This was great advice, especially when I decided to change computer platforms. My PC files could be migrated to a new software program on my Mac via a GEDCOM and nothing was lost. When I discovered that I missed the charting features of my old PC program, I was able to move my files back again and take advantages of those options.

Bottom Line: Learn to use the GEDCOM transfer process and keep your information in fields that transfer easily between programs and across platforms.

If you are unhappy with your current genealogy software, do your homework before starting with a new program. Use this handy guide to help you evaluate programs and make the best possible decision.

Guide to Choosing Genealogy Database Software

☐ Talk with people in your local society; what are members using?

☐ Does your local society sponsor software users groups? For what software?

☐ What kind of software training is available locally?

☐ Does the software company offer webinars, tutorials, books, etc.?

☐ How extensive is the software support site?

☐ When was the last software update? How often are new versions released?

☐ Is there a User Forum? If so, read forum comments, questions, and answers. Learn about possible pitfalls before you take the leap.

☐ Make a list of your customary tasks; how does the software handle these chores?

☐ Download trial versions and spend time "test-driving" the programs.

☐ Does your local society or FamilySearch center have software installed that you can test-drive on their computers?

☐ Will your current computer meet the software system requirements?

☐ Will you need to upgrade your technology?

☐ How does the software handle imports and exports?

☐ Does the software company offer mobile versions for smartphones or tablets?

☐ What are the license restrictions? Will you have to purchase a copy for each computer you use (such as laptop and desktop machines)?

☐ How does the software handle source citations?

☐ Does the software allow media attachments? How difficult is it to add media links?

☐ See the following resources section for links to reviews and products.

RESOURCES

Genealogy Database Software

FOR PCS

Family Tree Maker **<www.ancestry.com>**

Legacy Family Tree **<www.legacyfamilytree.com>**

RootsMagic **<www.rootsmagic.com>**

FOR MAC

Family Tree Maker **<www.ancestry.com>**

MacFamilyTree **<www.syniumsoftware.com/macfamilytree>**

Reunion **<www.leisterpro.com>**

Genealogy Database Reviews

Technology changes at lightning speed with new software versions and features announced all the time. Take advantage of the most recent reviews when researching your genealogy database options. These sites have proven to be reliable resources for information:

Genealogy at About.com **<www.genealogy.about.com>**

GenSoftReviews **<www.gensoftreviews.com>**

Genealogy Tools **< www.genealogytools.com>**

Top Ten Reviews **<www.genealogy-software-review.toptenreviews.com>**
GeneaMusings **<www.geneamusings.com>**
Cyndi's List **<www.cyndislist.com/software/genealogy>**

Genealogy Software

CENSUS TOOLS by Gary Minder **<www.censustools.com>**
A collection of spreadsheet templates for recording U.S. Federal and state census, international census, cemetery data, passenger manifest lists, research log, family group report. Microsoft Excel templates can be used to input your own data in your spreadsheet program. PDF forms are also included that may be printed out and completed by hand.

THE FAMILY HISTORY RESEARCH TOOLKIT by Michael Hait
<www.haitfamilyresearch.com/toolkit.aspx>
Forms and charts for genealogical research in typeable PDF format that can be used on any computer with Adobe Reader. The collection includes: family group record, pedigree chart, research log, U.S. Federal census extraction forms, household tracker forms, and several miscellaneous forms. These are typeable forms, not spreadsheet templates.

TRANSCRIPT 2.3 (PC) by Jacob Boerema **<www.jacobboerema.nl/en>**
Windows transcription software for working with handwritten documents. Features allow users to magnify, increase contrast, and clarify images.

Essential Software for Genealogists

TechTips **<www.familysearch.org/techtips>**
Digital Toolbox at Moultrie Creek Gazette **<www.moultriecreek.us>**

BOOKMARKING
Diigo **<www.diigo.com>**
Evernote **<www.evernote.com>**

CALENDAR AND TASK MANAGER
Google Calendar **<www.google.com/calendar>**
Microsoft Outlook **<www.microsoft.com/en=us/outlook>**
Apple iCal **<www.apple.com>**
Wunderlist **<www.wunderlist.com>**
Remember the Milk **<www.rememberthemilk.com>**

CLOUD STORAGE, SYNCING AND BACKUP

Amazon Cloud Drive **<www.amazon.com/clouddrive/learnmore>**

Apple iCloud **<www.apple.com/icloud/>**

Carbonite **<www.carbonite.com>**

Dropbox **<www.dropbox.com>**

Google Docs **<google.com/docs>**

Mozy **<www.mozy.com>**

Windows Live Skydrive **<explore.live.com>**

DATABASE

Microsoft Access **<www.microsoft.com>**

FileMaker, Bento 4 **<www.filemaker.com>**

DEVONthink **<www.devontechnologies.com>**

E-MAIL

Google Gmail **<www.mail.google.com>**

Microsoft Outlook **<www.microsoft.com>**

Apple Mail **<www.apple.com>**

NOTETAKING

DEVONnote **<www.devontechnologies.com>**

Evernote **<www.evernote.com>**

Microsoft OneNote **<www.microsoft.com>**

OFFICE SUITE

Microsoft Office **<www.microsoft.com>**

OpenOffice **<www.openoffice.org>**

Apple iWork **<www.apple.com/iwork>**

PHOTO ORGANIZING, EDITING AND SHARING

Adobe Photoshop Elements, Adobe Lightroom **<www.adobe.com>**

Apple iPhoto, Aperture **<www.apple.com>**

Flickr **<www.flickr.com>**

Google Picasa **<www.picasa.google.com>**

WEB BROWSER

Google Chrome **<www.google.com/chrome>**

Mozilla Firefox **<www.mozilla.org>**

Safari **<www.apple.com/safari>**

Microsoft Internet Explorer **<www.windows.microsoft.com>**

16

Organize and Discover Research Connections Online

When I started The Family Curator blog in 2008, my intention was simply to record my own journey of discovery as I unraveled the story of my grandmother's life. Arline's photos, letters, and documents were all waiting to reveal individual threads that could be rewoven into a beautiful and rich fabric. I knew that each precious thread might be the golden one, the life of the tale, and it was essential to move slowly and deliberately as I worked.

Making connections online through blogs, newsgroups, and social media sites is the new telephone party line. Someone reads something on the Internet that links to something else that links again to something else. It's one big, and very active, community party line, and you don't need anyone's permission to cut in!

Genealogists know that our ancestors didn't live their lives in isolation. Most often, our ancestors were part of families, neighborhoods, and towns. They interacted regularly and more intimately with many people in a way that we might find intrusive in our modern, anonymous lifestyles today. Neighbors probably knew as much (or more) about each other than extended family members did. A good researcher will try to tap into these extended networks when building the life story and family tree of his ancestors. This chapter will help you organize the time and energy you spend online so you can effectively and efficiently connect with fellow researchers whether they are across town, across the country, or around the world.

MAKE CONNECTIONS WITH BLOGS

Genealogy blogs are one of the fastest-growing information portals for family historians. Hundreds of researchers post new stories and photos daily about their ancestors; they are looking for new connections, and they aren't hard to find.

The world of genealogy bloggers, or GeneaBloggers, is cataloged and indexed by Web-crawlers that can find a "hit" to your online search. Start by locating blogs that cover families or topics of interest to you. Search for family surname, locality, organizations, and ethnicity. Get started with the master genealogy blog list maintained by Thomas MacEntee at Geneabloggers **<www.geneabloggers.com>**.

Use a Blog Reader

As you build a list of blogs to follow, you will need a way to manage your new reading material. It's too time consuming to visit each blog address every day to check for new posts. One of the best, and easiest, methods is to use a blog reader. Instead of going to individual blogs to read new posts, a blog reader brings new posts to you so you can check just one Web page and see all of the updates in one place.

The free Google Reader application is a good place to start. You will need a free Google Account.

1. Go to Google.com and register for a free account **<www.accounts.google.com>**.
2. Go to a blog you would like to regularly read and look for the Subscribe or RSS button. It's usually a large orange button.
3. Click on the orange RSS button to subscribe to the blog.
4. Follow the prompts to "Subscribe" to the blog.
5. To read new posts, open Google Reader from the Google menu bar at the top of any Google page, and scroll through the feeds from your favorite blogs.

RESEARCH WHILE YOU SLEEP WITH GOOGLE ALERTS

Wouldn't it be nice if you opened your e-mail inbox and found new cousin connections waiting for you? The Google Alert feature can be configured to work while you sleep, searching the Internet for anything you need.

1. Sign in to your Google Account and go to the Google Alerts page **<www.google.com/alerts>**.
2. Fill in the box with your Search query. To minimize wild hits, place names in quotation marks: "Annie Smith." Set queries using variations of names as well: "Annie Jean Smith" and "Ann J. Smith."
3. Choose what kind of sources to include in your search; you will probably want to leave this at Everything.
4. Set the frequency for notifications. Options are: as it happens, once a day, once a week.
5. Select how many results to return. Options are: all or only the best.
6. Choose your delivery option.

Use the Manage Alert button to add more alerts or make changes to existing alerts. Other uses for Google Alerts include:

• Track your own name and your blog title to keep up with what folks say about you.
• Watch for family material that may come up for auction. Use Surnames with the word *Bible, photo, letter.*
• Follow research topics of interest.
• Follow news about a conference or event.

MAKE CONNECTIONS ONLINE

Caution: Don't try this unless you are ready to meet new people, learn new stories, and maybe even increase the size of your family archive. Making connections online can have unexpected results! The World Wide Web is filled with surprises. Post a nice juicy tidbit of information in a corner of the Web and wait to see what gets caught.

Just how do you make connections online? Is it hard? Is it scary? Will people find out about my private life? Security and privacy are probably the biggest concerns for people looking to make connections online. It's a circular dilemma: We want to find family and friends, but we don't want to reveal too much about ourselves unintentionally, and not until we are ready to do so.

Use these guidelines and helpful resources to help you manage your online presence:

Checklist for Online Privacy

• **DO NOT USE THE SAME USERNAME AND PASSWORD ON ALL SITES.** Use a password manager to create and manage multiple logins, or create a personal system that you can remember. (See the chapter five resources section for password management software.)
• **KNOW HOW TO CONTROL YOUR PRIVACY SETTINGS**. When enrolling in a new social media site, read the Terms of Service and Privacy guidelines.
• **AVOID POSTING SPECIFIC INFORMATION ABOUT VACATIONS.** If you are worried about home security, don't broadcast the dates when your house will be vacant.
• **BE WARY OF POSTING TOO MUCH INFORMATION ABOUT YOUNG CHILDREN.** Never expose the children you love to the eyes of a possible lurker with less-than-honorable intentions. Send the cute bath-time photos to grandma in a private e-mail. Never post school or vacation information.
• **POST ONLY INFORMATION YOU ARE COMFORTABLE SHARING WITH STRANGERS.** Protect yourself by only posting information that you would give to anyone. Social media sites expose your words to friends, and friends of friends. It's easy to lose track of everyone who may read about your morning breakfast. The safest route is to only post information you would freely give to anyone at all.

Use a Persona

I was tied in knots about privacy issues when I first became active online. Creating The Family Curator identity gave me some sense of anonymity, but as I grew more comfortable adjusting privacy settings and posting content, I added my real name. Some folks think of a pseudonym as something "only writers" do, but anyone can adopt a new identity to use online. The biggest catch is that by using a pseudonym, those cousins you're looking for may never find you.

If you are uncomfortable revealing your true identity online, consider using an online persona, an alias to present yourself to the world. Choose a nickname or business name; reveal as much or as little as you wish.

Start With Forums, Bulletin Boards, and LIST-SERVs

Message boards and forums have been around since the earliest days of the Internet. Typically managed by an organization or website, these online services allow interaction between members, sometimes within a closed environment. Other sites are open to the public and can be read by anyone.

For instance, if you register on a website forum with a username GeniLady24 giving your Gmail account, it's pretty tough for anyone to actually discover your real name and address unless you share it. Unfortunately, you and your potential connections need to both be using the same website, and this makes it harder to find folks.

Helpful forums for genealogists include:

Ancestry.com Message Boards **<www.boards.ancestry.com>**

Cyndi's List Queries & Message Boards **<www.cyndislist.com/queries>**

NEHGS Discussion Board, at American Ancestors, The New England Historic Genealogical Society Website **<www.americanancestors.org/discussions.aspx>**

Genealogy.com GenForum **<www.genforum.com>**

Follow these tips to increase your chances of success on these sites

☐ Post at the biggest, most popular sites, or at specific sites relevant to your search.

☐ Only post information you are willing to share with the world at large.

☐ Protect your identity with a username that does not include your real name.

☐ Post one well-crafted query on the message board most closely related to the information you seek. If you post the same query on every board in a forum, people may think you are a "spammer" and not respond.

WRITE A QUERY THAT GETS RESULTS

The genealogy queries once placed in magazines are now posted online in forums and message boards. Which post would you be more likely to read and respond to? *I'm looking for my grandmother. Her name was Bessie Smith.* Or *Seeking information about BESSIE (MILLER)*

SMITH b.1895 Muscotah, Atchison Co., KS, m. 1820 Herman Smith of Kansas City, Jackson Co., MO b. 1890. No other information. I would like to connect with others researching the BESSIE MILLER or HERMAN SMITH families. Please contact me at [e-mail address].

When writing a query to post on forums, message boards, or LIST-SERVs, include the surname in your subject line and all pertinent information:

☐ full name, including any middle initials or maiden names

☐ birth, marriage, and death dates (use abbreviations b-m-d if desired)

☐ places where events occurred

☐ any known residences

☐ names of spouse, children, parents

☐ your contact information

☐ what you want to know

Set up a free online e-mail account, such as Gmail **<mail.google.com>**, Yahoo! **<mail.yahoo.com>**, or Hotmail **<hotmail.com>** and use this account as the contact information for all online queries. This separate account has two purposes:

1. It protects your privacy.

2. You can keep this account for years and years, even if you switch Internet service providers. Queries stay online for a very long time, and you want people to be able to contact you even if the post is several years old.

CONNECT WITH FAMILY THROUGH SOCIAL MEDIA SITES

Online message boards, forums, and LIST-SERVs are the "old-timers" of the social media world. New "upstarts" like Facebook and Google+ steal a lot of attention these days, but don't let the commotion make you feel left out of the party. Participate at the level where you are most comfortable, then stretch yourself to try new ways to connect with people as you gain experience and expertise.

Review the Checklist for Online Privacy and consider joining popular social media websites to connect with family and friends.

Facebook <www.facebook.com>

What started as a college photo yearbook has grown into a social networking phenomenon where grandparents post as often as teens. Facebook can be hard to define: microblogging, photo sharing, and instant news are all hallmarks of this fast-paced program.

If you aren't sure whether or not Facebook is for you, ask a FB (Facebook) Friend to let you look over his or her shoulder to see what all the fuss is about. Search for your local genealogy society to see if it has a Facebook page. Look for old high school friends or family members.

Google+ <www.google.com>

The Internet giant Google created a unique version of social networking with Google+. At first, many people thought it would be "just another" Facebook, but Google+ has turned out to be a different kind of social media. I've heard it said: If Facebook is a party with everyone chattering at once about all kinds of things, Google+ is a meeting of like-minded members where people stick to the topic at hand.

Google+ is organized so that you can join Groups made up of people who share similar interests, whether that be genealogy, military history, knitting, or your local Rotary Club. Groups cut down on the chatter and noise, resulting in a more focused conversation between members.

Flickr <www.flickr.com>

Online photo sharing has become just as popular with genealogists as microblogging sites like Facebook and Google+, and it's easy to see why. Families and clubs post event photos, professionals and artists showcase their latest projects, and The Library of Congress brings its collection to the public on Flickr.

Like other social media sites, when you join Flickr, you will be able to customize your privacy settings and build an online persona. Start out with a small collection of photos and let it grow. Easy integration with smartphone cameras and digital photo programs make it easy to upload photos and manage your Flickr account.

Twitter <www.twitter.com>

If some social media sites are known for microblogging, Twitter must be nanoblogging. This fast-moving service allows users to post updates, news, and links no longer than 140 characters. That's not a lot of space, but it's proven to be more than enough to send late-breaking world news and remarkable updates.

Twitter's small-scale interface works especially well for updates at conferences, or to let your friends know where they can find you at an event.

LibraryThing <www.librarything.com>

Books are the new "big thing" in social networking, with LibraryThing opening the doors to some of the most interesting personal libraries in the world. Do you want to know what books line the shelves of your favorite genealogist's office? Look for their name on LibraryThing and take a peek.

Family history often requires research with esoteric and hard-to-find books; use LibraryThing to find the title and ask the owner for a lookup. Read peer reviews before you make new purchases. Get recommendations for a good basic genealogy library or find new volumes to fill in your own shelves. You may be surprised at the people you find at LibraryThing.

TRACKING QUERIES AND RESPONSES

To manage information you find through message boards and social media sites, you will need an effective system to track posts, queries, and results. I suggest adding to a system you already use, rather than implementing something new.

If you are an Evernote **<www.evernote.com>** fan, add tags for each of your social media sites. Use the Web clipping feature to clip and save your original query and any responses. Be sure to add tags for surnames or topics so you can find your posts later.

DEVONthink **<www.devontechnologies.com>** works much like Evernote, without the need for Internet access. Integrate your social media clips with your general research for efficient and all-inclusive searching.

If you prefer tracking information with tables or spreadsheets, build your own social media log to manage queries and responses. Remember to add dates, url addresses, and contact information. See chapter ten for ideas on organizing with Information Managers.

RESOURCES

Blogs and Blogging

GeneaBloggers, by Thomas MacEntee **<www.geneabloggers.com>**

Become a Genealogy Blog Reader Webinar, by Thomas MacEntee **<www.hidefgen.com/presentations/genealogy-blog-reader/>**

Books

Discover your Family History Online by Nancy Hendrickson
The Genealogist's Google Toolbox by Lisa Louise Cooke
Social Networking for Genealogists by Drew Smith

Message Boards and Forums

Ancestry.com Message Boards **<www.boards.ancestry.com>**

Cyndi's List Queries & Message Boards **<www.cyndislist.com/queries>**

NEHGS Discussion Board, at American Ancestors, The New England Historic Genealogical Society Website **<www.americanancestors.org/discussions.aspx>**

Genealogy.com GenForum **<www.genforum.com>**

Conclusion

Inheriting a family archive can be a blessing or a burden. Along with the heirloom jewelry, china, old letters, and documents, our ancestors' faces look back at us from faded photographs, sometimes seeming to say with a stare, "Don't forget me."

I've never had any trouble saving things, but as my home archive groans with growing pains, I realize that I just can't save everything. My grandmother would never want me to throw out my son's stamp collection to make room for crumbling newspapers. I am beginning to investigate archives that might welcome my family heritage collection. With the advent of digitization, I can still work with the information and free my family from the physical burden of managing the entire archive.

I do know that I will never part with some things—Arline's baptismal certificate, the only record of her birth; the lovely photograph of her at eighteen; and at least some of the letters Mom and I enjoyed reading together. Those things I still want to feel, and smell, and touch.

How you choose to care for your family archive will depend on your personal situation, your lifestyle, and your own plans for the future. We're fortunate to live in a time when technology offers alternatives to losing an old letter or a fading photograph. With care and foresight we can continue as good stewards of our family legacy and make new memories for our own descendants.

I wish you many happy hours discovering the treasures in your own family archive. I'd love to hear about your experiences with the techniques in this book and the treasures you find; please send me a note at familycurator@gmail.com.

Happy archiving!

Denise Levenick
Pasadena, California

ACKNOWLEDGMENTS

This book began over a century ago when my grandmother Arline and her sister Mercy were captivated by the notion that two dirt-poor Kansas farm girls could be related to British royalty. The photographs, documents, pedigree charts, and query letters they saved tell a story of curiosity and persistence that was still largely incomplete when my mother, Suzanne, and her sister Frances inherited the archive. Locked away in a trunk for decades, the bits and pieces are now left to my sister and me to finally pull together into a tale for our children. As that story finds its way to print, I am grateful that the Winsor women had the care and foresight to preserve the heirloom documents of our family. My love and appreciation goes to them all, especially Auntie for her care of Arline's trunk.

My strategy for a family archive grew in small steps, inspired by professional archivists, genealogists, and enthusiastic genealogy bloggers who generously shared their experience and expertise. Thank you Lisa Louise Cooke, Elyse Doerflinger, Sheri Fenley, Midge Frazel, A.C. Ivory, Sally Jacobs, Judy Lucey, Thomas MacEntee, Craig Manson, Denise Olson, Randy Seaver, and Maureen Taylor.

I am especially grateful to the readers of The Family Curator for their comments, questions, and lively discussion on so many family treasures and archival puzzles. I learn something new from you every day!

Thank you, thank you to footnoteMaven who first spied a bigger story in my journey and urged me to "tell more" for *Shades of the Departed* online magazine. One story turned into another, and then a new column as Miss Penelope Dreadful was born.

I want to thank my blogging-buddy Amy Coffin for holding me accountable with our annual meet-ups, and coach Nancy Hendrickson for helping me figure out what to do next.

Many thanks to Publisher Allison Dolan for our enjoyable "pitch sessions" and for her confidence in me with this topic. It's a true pleasure to work with Allison and editors like Diane Haddad, Kerry Scott, and Jackie Musser at *Family Tree Magazine*, whose ideas and enthusiasm help keep writer's block at bay.

And, because genealogists know "it's all about the family," thank you to my family for their continued encouragement and support: my Dad, Ed; Polly; Dede; and Kip. My sons, Zack and Christian, and their families cheered on my progress, reminding me why we want to save our family treasures, and nephew John and Co. provided a New England home base for seasonal recharging. Most of all, I must thank my fellow-keeper-of-the-stuff, Mr. Curator, whose patience and optimism make any project possible.

ABOUT THE AUTHOR

Denise Levenick has written about organizing, preserving, and sharing family treasures at her blog The Family Curator **<www.theFamilyCurator.com>** since 2008, twice voted one of the 40 Best Genealogy Blogs. She is a frequent contributor to *Family Tree Magazine* and webinar presenter for Family Tree University, and an enthusiastic speaker on archival topics. Denise is a native Southern Californian and lives in a historic home in Pasadena, California with her husband and a growing family archive. Visit her at **<www.theFamilyCurator.com>**.

DEDICATION

This book is dedicated to my mother, Suzanne Mercy Winsor Brown, who always believed there was a story inside Arline's trunk waiting for me to write it down;

And to my husband, Dan . . .

Mom was right again when she said you were "a keeper."

ISBN: 978-1-4403-2223-5

Other Family Tree Books are available from your local bookstore and online suppliers.
For more genealogy resources, visit **<shopfamilytree.com>**.

16 15 14 13 12   5 4 3 2 1

DISTRIBUTED IN CANADA BY FRASER DIRECT
100 Armstrong Avenue
Georgetown, Ontario, Canada L7G 5S4
Tel: (905) 877-4411

DISTRIBUTED IN THE U.K. AND EUROPE BY
F&W Media International, LTD
Brunel House, Forde Close,
Newton Abbot, TQ12 4PU, UK
Tel: (+44) 1626 323200,
Fax (+44) 1626 323319
E-mail: enquiries@fwmedia.com

DISTRIBUTED IN AUSTRALIA BY CAPRICORN LINK
P.O. Box 704, Windsor, NSW 2756 Australia
Tel: (02) 4577-3555

PUBLISHER/EDITORIAL DIRECTOR: Allison Dolan
EDITOR: Jacqueline Musser
DESIGNER: Julie Barnett
PRODUCTION COORDINATOR: Debbie Thomas

FREE DOWNLOAD
CHECKLISTS, CHARTS & FORMS

Download free digital copies of the checklists, charts and forms that appear in this book. Print multiple copies for your use or type directly in the forms. Visit <familytreeuniversity.com/familykeepsakes> for your free downloads.

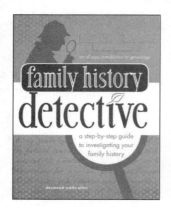
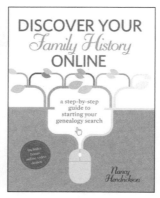